I COULD BE WRONG, BUT I DOUBT IT

ALSO BY PHIL ROBERTSON

Happy, Happy, Happy
UnPHILtered
The Theft of America's Soul
Jesus Politics
Uncanceled

I COULD BE WRONG, BUT I DOUBT IT

*Why Jesus Is Your Greatest Hope
on Earth and in Eternity*

PHIL ROBERTSON

WITH GORDON DASHER

**NELSON
BOOKS**

An Imprint of Thomas Nelson

Published in Nashville, Tennessee, by Nelson Books, an imprint of Thomas Nelson. Nelson Books and Thomas Nelson are registered trademarks of HarperCollins Christian Publishing, Inc.

Published in association with Yates & Yates, www.yates2.com.

Thomas Nelson titles may be purchased in bulk for educational, business, fundraising, or sales promotional use. For information, please email SpecialMarkets@ThomasNelson.com.

Unless otherwise noted, Scripture quotations are taken from The Holy Bible, New International Version®, NIV®. Copyright © 1973, 1978, 1984, 2011 by Biblica, Inc.® Used by permission of Zondervan. All rights reserved worldwide. www.Zondervan.com. The "NIV" and "New International Version" are trademarks registered in the United States Patent and Trademark Office by Biblica, Inc.®

Scripture quotations marked CEB are taken from the Common English Bible. Copyright © 2011 Common English Bible.

Scripture quotations marked KJV are taken from the King James Version. Public domain.

Scripture quotations marked MSG [or THE MESSAGE] are taken from THE MESSAGE. Copyright © 1993, 2002, 2018 by Eugene H. Peterson. Used by permission of NavPress. All rights reserved. Represented by Tyndale House Publishers, a Division of Tyndale House Ministries.

Scripture quotations marked NET are taken from the NET Bible® copyright ©1996–2017 by Biblical Studies Press, L.L.C. http://netbible.com. All rights reserved.

Scripture quotations marked NKJV are taken from the New King James Version®. Copyright © 1982 by Thomas Nelson. Used by permission. All rights reserved.

Scripture quotations marked NLT are taken from the Holy Bible, New Living Translation. Copyright © 1996, 2004, 2015 by Tyndale House Foundation. Used by permission of Tyndale House Ministries, Carol Stream, Illinois 60188. All rights reserved.

Any internet addresses, phone numbers, or company or product information printed in this book are offered as a resource and are not intended in any way to be or to imply an endorsement by Thomas Nelson, nor does Thomas Nelson vouch for the existence, content, or services of these sites, phone numbers, companies, or products beyond the life of this book.

ISBN 978-1-4002-3018-1 (HC)
ISBN 978-1-4002-3022-8 (ePub)
ISBN 978-1-4002-4962-6 (custom)

Library of Congress Control Number: 2023951360

Printed in the United States of America
24 25 26 27 28 LBC 5 4 3 2 1

To my mother, Merritt Robertson, who—despite her personal struggle with mental health—taught me to love God. Whatever passion I have for sharing the love of God with others I learned from watching her. Thank you, Ma!

CONTENTS

INTRODUCTION

ackbreaking work! That's what I used to say after a hard day's work brushing duck blinds or working on my tractor. But I was a young man then. Very young. To be honest, I had no idea then what I was talking about. I didn't know what backbreaking work was until I actually broke my back while working.

It was a twenty-foot-long aluminum boat with a mud motor weighing hundreds of pounds attached to the transom. Dan the Butler and I were struggling to launch it in shallow water. Yours truly had the bright idea of placing our backs against the bow of the boat and manhandling it into the water. "One, two, three, *push!*"

That's when I heard the crack. It is also when I felt a sharp burning pain in the middle of my back. I have never been pierced in my spine with a knife, but the first thought I had was, *I've been stabbed!* Staggering back toward my vehicle, I groaned to old Dan through my gritted teeth, "I've done it now."

The doctor was blunt. "You have fractured a vertebra." Then he added insult to injury: "Phil, you do know that you are seventy-six years old, don't you? It's time you accepted reality."

A week after they cemented the broken bone back together, I bent down to retrieve a bottle of propane from the concrete floor of my cook shed and felt another piece of my spine pop. Surgery number two! Am I falling apart, or what?

The doctor was a bit apologetic about it, but he was right. I am officially a member of the geriatric-old-man club, no doubt about it. After a lifetime of pretending that old age would not catch up to me, the reality finally dawned: I am a young man trapped in a declining and aging physical body.

I try to look on the bright side of things, but it is difficult to find anything positive about pieces of your skeletal framework fracturing.

If anything good came out of my coming face-to-face with old age, it was the stark reminder that we aren't on this planet for very long. It may be difficult for you young bucks to comprehend this, but the time between my teenage years and now has been very brief. The Bible calls life a "vapor" (James 4:14 NKJV). Some translations say it's a "mist." However you translate that word, I would agree with any word that communicates extreme brevity. It's over in a flash!

All I can tell you is that it has gone by so fast it baffles me, shocks me. But coming to terms with it has compelled me to reflect even more on my mortality and to consider what comes next. And it has given me a certain urgency about the years I have left.

Since, without exception, we are all going to die, I'm thinking that we all need to ponder the fact that death is inevitable. I mean, if it is inevitable, we might want to prepare for it, right?

So, let me ask you a question: Are you going to die? Have you given much thought to the reality that you have an expiration date?

You and I may not like to think about it. We may even try to stave off the inevitable with pharmaceuticals and surgeries and extreme workouts, but the cold, hard facts are undeniable: a day is looming on the horizon for all of us when we will take our last gasp of air. After that, it's all over for us as far as life on this planet is concerned.

In my last book, *Uncanceled*, I told my readers about a young man who became enraged when I suggested he would die one day. He stormed out of the house in a fit of rage, screaming at the top of his voice, "No one is going to tell me I'm going to die. I will live forever!" He was stabbed to death in a bar fight less than a month later.

What a sad story. I wish he had listened to the Word of God that plainly tells us what we already know: we will not escape the grim reaper. Not one of us will. Our appointment with death is inescapable. All of humanity has a disease, and that disease's mortality rate is 100 percent.

Is this topic the best way to introduce my book or what?

You may shudder at the thought. It is a sobering topic for discussion over afternoon coffee. I'll admit that. But we can't avoid it. So, I just figure it's best to confront it.

But I've got good news for you. I believe there's a hope that's bigger—much bigger—than the tragedy of death.

I don't know when I will die, but I can tell you this: the date of my demise looms larger and larger as I draw nearer to it. I can also assure you that I detest aging. I enjoyed many years where my body never failed me. But now? Well, let's just say that I will be modifying my physical activity in an effort to retain some kind of mobility.

Even though I don't like aging, and even though I don't like the idea that my body will cease to exist in its present form, I am not in despair. Not even a little bit. I still live with purpose. I am completely fulfilled. I am still a joyful man. All of the time!

If you are wondering how an aging man whose body is beginning to fail him could say something like that, let me take you back to the year I turned twenty-eight. Until then, I had been a self-absorbed, hedonistic, evil man who lived for one purpose: to please my inner man—the selfish man, Phil Robertson. I didn't care about Miss Kay, my boys, or anyone else. I wanted to do what I wanted to do, and I set out to accomplish just that. If anything stood in the way of my realizing my goal of self-gratification, I simply pushed it out of my way and relentlessly pursued the fine art of pleasing myself. I lived by the mantra that was popular back in the sixties and seventies, "If it feels good, do it!"

But a funny thing happened on my way to a party. I've told this story before, but it's worth retelling here. My sister Jan and her pastor, Bill Smith, had other plans for me because they knew the Almighty had other plans for me. They were well aware of my daily appointment with the Evil One, Satan. They knew I was, without a doubt, under his control. However, they also knew if I could just meet their best friend, my life could be radically different.

So, they brought their friend into the bar I owned in Junction City, Arkansas, and let him speak to me. I couldn't see him because he was living inside of them, but he was there. I have no doubt about that now. And when they brought him to me, I finally listened to what he had to say about my life and what he had done for me. I say the brevity of my life shocks me, but that shock is nothing compared to the shock of meeting Jesus. From that day on, I was a changed man.

After I had a head-on collision with the one who claims to be "'the way, the truth, and the life'" (John 14:6 NKJV), I couldn't go on living the way I had been up to that point. For the first time in my life, my desperation was replaced with hope. My fear was replaced with love. Rather than dreading death, I began to enjoy a new life rooted in an eternal future.

In other words, I put on immortality. The apostle Paul described my transformation two thousand years before it happened:

> Listen, I tell you a mystery: We will not all sleep, but we will all be changed—in a flash, in the twinkling of an eye, at the last trumpet. For the trumpet will sound, the dead will be raised imperishable, and we will be changed. For the perishable must clothe itself with the imperishable, and the mortal with immortality. (1 Cor. 15:51–53)

I guess you could say death was finally off the table for me. Yes, I knew my body would eventually die and rot in the ground, but Jesus was offering me freedom from the permanence of the grave. If he is who he claimed to be, and if he's telling the truth, then following him was a no-brainer. On the day that I believed in him, I clothed my perishable body with the future imperishable body. My mortal body was covered by the promise of eternal life. He promised to raise my dead body from the ground. So, I went with Jesus the rest of the way.

I've lived that way ever since. Everything in us cries out that death is unnatural, that it isn't supposed to be this way, but it will still happen to all of us. Presidents, kings and queens, rock stars, as well as the guy who hooks up your cable and the waitress at the Waffle House will all perish. But I don't fear it because of what Jesus has done to reverse the finality of it.

You know I'm telling the truth about death. So, I have a simple question: What are you going to do about it? I have a plan, and that plan's name is Jesus. What's your strategy for getting out of the grave?

I ask because, as far as I can tell, you only have two choices, and those choices are directly linked to what you believe to be true about the origin of life. What I mean is, either we are here as a result of blind chance or someone put us here. Either we evolved from matter that just happened to appear billions of years ago (for no reason at all) or God created all that we see, including you!

Both views of our origin have consequences. Very different consequences! If we are just here because we are here, that means there's nothing else after the grave. We live a little while, and then we die. Our bodies are buried or burned, but there's nothing after that. We're like a mushroom that pops up from a rotting log and lives for a few days, only to die and be absorbed back into the ecosystem.

Unfortunately, if the naturalistic, unguided, godless theory of the origin of the universe is true, then you and I are no more important or valuable or significant than that mushroom. We exist, yes, but there is no real purpose to our existence. There's no objective moral code or meaning to life. We will die and our bodies will decompose and be absorbed back into the earth.

End of story! End of you! And me! And all of humanity! It will be as if we never lived.

Bleak? Well, yes, it's bleak! It is a sad tale with horrifying consequences because it reduces us all to atoms and molecules. Nothing more!

Sadly, if this view of life is true, no amount of wishing it were not true would change the reality of it. We can dupe ourselves with stories of gods and saviors and redemption, but if God isn't there, and we just popped up on the scene for no reason at all, we'll just have to live with it—until we don't anymore.

There is only one outcome for the man or woman who believes this story about the origins of life and confronts the implications of it head-on: *despondency*! This story offers no hope, no objective reason for the pursuit of anything good or for the avoidance of evil because in a world like this, good and evil don't even exist.

You live, then you die, and after that, nothing. Not one second of any of your days on earth had any real meaning at all.

But what if there is another narrative that is both real and hopeful? What if there was another story that told of a God who created us, loved us, died for us, and was raised from the dead for us? What if you knew that this star-breathing, death-defeating God also promises you immortality in exchange for you simply believing in him? For trusting him?

I'm not saying that we should accept the story of hope found in the God narrative simply because the other story is so bleak. As I said, if that other bleak story reflects reality, then it is what it is. No god myth will change that!

My purpose in writing this book, however, is to stimulate something in you that will cause you to consider the possibility that the God narrative is the real story for why we are here. If it's true, you would want to know about it, wouldn't you?

If the bleak, meaningless story about the beginning of the universe is true, and my faith in God as the Creator is nothing more than a fairy tale, guess what? We will all wind up in the same place—in nothingness. None of our whining about justice or injustice, wrongdoing, failed government policies, elections, or conspiracy theories will matter.

However, what if my story is true?

What if you could live out your life on earth with eternal purpose?

What if your fear and dread about your mortality could be put in the context of the promise of immortality?

What if God really is there? What if he actually raised Jesus from the dead and promises to do the same for those who put their trust in him?

Would you want in on it?

If your answer is no, maybe you should put this book down and return it for a refund. But if you answered yes, then I suggest you keep on reading. I'm going to tell the story of a real God who offers real hope.

I wanted to write this book because I had this thought that Jesus is really making his case, from Genesis to Revelation, that he is not only qualified to be the master of our lives, but that he desires to be. We don't like to think about God begging, but he does plead with us to come to him.

If you are uncomfortable with the idea that God pleads with humankind to embrace immortality, I would encourage you to look at the parable of the prodigal son in Luke 15. There, the father, who represents God the Father in this parable, pleads with the older son to join the party celebrating his brother's return to the family (v. 28).

But aside from the father's plea to the older brother, this parable is a perfect example of a father whose deepest desire is for his son to return to the family. When I read this story, I see a father who longs for his child's presence. He yearns for him. The passage doesn't say specifically, but it hints at the possibility that the father spent his days scanning the horizon, anticipating the young man's homecoming.

> "But while he was still a long way off, his father saw him and was filled with compassion for him; he ran to his son, threw his arms around him and kissed him." (v. 20)

He saw him from a great distance and ran out to meet him. The boy had pursued a deadly lifestyle by squandering the intimate relationship he had with his father. In spite of that, the father still pined for his boy. Not only that, but he was also quick to forgive the lad; he wouldn't even entertain the son's prepared speech. He simply wiped away the son's past and poured out his love on him.

God pleading with his children to embrace immortality? What a novel idea! Who would dream up a god like that?

That's good news if you're a wretched sinner like me. I was the prodigal son. And sometimes I have been the unforgiving older son too. Each of them made choices that would lead to death, but the father only wanted one thing: to give them life.

But the news gets even better. Jesus has left a trail of evidence in the Scriptures that gives us a better understanding of who he is. I call the Bible "the résumé of Jesus." One attribute of Christ after another is laid out for us to see, and these truths enable us to come to the conclusion that Jesus alone is qualified to offer us real hope for both the present and the future. Everything is written to enable us to conclude that he is up to the job. We can trust him!

And in choosing him, we are choosing life—eternal life. Immortality! But the life we are choosing is far more than simply avoiding hell or annihilation in favor of living on gold-paved streets that begin at a pearly gate. We are choosing an intimate future in the presence of the Father we love and the Son who died for us and was raised from the dead on our behalf.

I don't know about you, but I can't wait for the day when my faith is made real (Heb. 11:1). That's because on that day, the loss of my parents and five of my siblings, the broken bones in my back, the rapid onset of old age, war, and the political unrest that has America by the throat will be overwhelmed by the goodness of eternity. I'll look back across the divide between time and eternity and say with the apostle Paul,

> Where, O death, is your victory?
> Where, O death, is your sting? (1 Cor. 15:55)

Resurrection from the dead? My lifeless body reassembled and given new life again? Rising up to meet the returning Savior in the air? Going to a place he has prepared for me where I will live with him forever?

When I heard that story, I said, "I'm all in!" And I continue to say the same thing every day. Age and death continue to stun me, but in my inner being, I anticipate Resurrection Day with passionate desire. I can't wait to experience it.

I'm not pleading with you to accept my story just because it's a better story. What I am asking you to do is to give it a once-over. Check it out for yourself. Examine the claims Scripture makes about Jesus and find out whether they're true. Is he who he claims to be? I have answered that question for myself, but I can't answer it for you. Only you can do that.

The reason I make this plea is that, in my experience, people who know Jesus and take him at his word about how they should live during their brief time here on earth tend to invest in things that are permanent rather than temporary. Jesus people tend to engage in delayed gratification. They have evaluated the things of this world and compared them to the things of heaven and concluded it is far better to invest in eternal things.

Jesus himself pointed out how important it is to correctly evaluate and prioritize things:

> "Do not store up for yourselves treasures on earth, where moths and vermin destroy, and where thieves break in and steal. But store up for yourselves treasures in heaven, where moths and vermin do not destroy, and where thieves do not break in and steal. For where your treasure is, there your heart will be also." (Matt. 6:19–21)

Here's a filter I put my stuff through: If anything I own or anything I'm inclined to invest my time and energy into, including my own life, is capable of being eaten by moths, worms, vermin, or oxidation, it goes on the bottom of my list of important stuff. If it won't stand the test of time, why would I waste my time with it. I've had plenty of stuff, to be honest with you. Outboard motors, boats, vehicles, houses, land, and a little bit of money. Unfortunately for those who think this stuff will add quality to their lives, it won't. That's because not a bit of it will last. It won't stand the test of time, and it sure won't stand the test of eternity.

Thankfully, there is something that will endure for eternity, and it goes on the top of my list. And that "thing" is Jesus!

The Gospel of John is an excellent outline for what we are talking about. Each of the chapters of this gospel presents a different quality of Jesus.

As I said, all I'm asking anyone to do is give it a fair look. Who knows? Maybe there is a God who can restore sanity to your life and the community of humanity around the world.

At least I think it's worth looking into.

one

JESUS, THE CREATOR

*In the beginning was the Word, and the Word was
with God, and the Word was God. He was with God
in the beginning. Through him all things were made;
without him nothing was made that has been made.*

JOHN 1:1–3

What's your top speed? I mean, what's the fastest you've ever
traveled from one place to the next? Back in the day, I rode in
one of the fastest cars around in the late sixties: a 1969 Pontiac GTO
model called The Judge that could reach top speeds of 158 mph.[1] That
was a rush.

As impressive as The Judge was in 1969, however, it moves like
a turtle when compared to many of the stock cars on the market
today. For example, the Tesla Model S Plaid can reach 60 mph in a

mind-boggling 1.9 seconds with top speeds of over 200 mph. Now, that's fast!

I've never ridden in a Tesla of any kind. As a matter of fact, I don't know if I've ever even seen one down here on the banks of the Ouachita River. It's not exactly suited for traversing the swampy river bottom that I call home, if you know what I mean.

But even if I had ridden in one of these lightning-fast Teslas, and even if the S Plaid had reached its top speed while I was in it, that would still fall far short of the fastest I've ever traveled.

As it turns out, at this very moment, I am going in circles at the unbelievable speed of one thousand miles per hour. Not only that, but this ball I'm riding on is hurtling through space at the blazing pace of sixty-seven thousand miles per hour as it orbits our star.

Now that is some serious speed. And not a hair is blown out of place. No sensation of speed or motion or anything. I'm just along for the ride, and I never give it a second thought. In fact, I'm not even aware of it.

Nope, you and I go about our daily business and don't even know that we are on the ride of a lifetime. I thought about this recently as my crew was lounging in a duck blind. Far off in the distance, I took note of a group of mallards making a beeline for our decoys. So, I did what I've done for at least sixty years of my life: I ordered everyone to hunker down and stay still.

But the truth of it was, we weren't still at all. We were hitching a ride on Planet Earth as it spun on its axis and blasted through space, but none of us were aware of it.

In spite of the fact that we often take for granted the laws of nature that control how this giant sphere behaves, the truth is that it is an impressive ball of rock when you stop and think about it. Precisely tilted on its axis and strategically placed just far enough from the sun to sustain life, this is an amazing place we call home base.

As cool as our planet is, when we contemplate the entire creation, it is a mind-blowing universe we live in. It's possible the question has never crossed your mind, but I have often wondered how it all got here.

That is a good question, wouldn't you agree? I only ask that because how you answer it determines how you live your life.

The Consequence of Benching God

As I said in the introduction, there are only two competing views: either someone put this together or no one did. The first view can give us a coherent view of how we got here and why we are here as well as what comes next. The second view leads to an empty and meaningless view of humanity. It just happened. No reason! We're just here.

I don't think anyone would argue that taking God out of our explanation of the universe has led to anything good. Even Friedrich Nietzsche, perhaps the most famous of atheists, admitted as much.

> God is dead. God remains dead. And we have killed him. How shall we comfort ourselves, the murderers of all murderers? . . . What water is there for us to clean ourselves? What festivals of atonement, what sacred games shall we have to invent? Is not the greatness of this deed too great for us? Must we ourselves not become gods simply to appear worthy of it?[2]

While Nietzsche was an unrepentant nonbeliever, I give him credit for recognizing the effects of killing off God. Without God, we don't have a moral code, we have no way to remove our sins, and we have no hope for our eternal future.

I've been around long enough to notice America's slow separation from God. In the 1960s, our teachers led us in prayer and Bible reading at the beginning of each school day. But in 1963, Madalyn Murray O'Hair convinced the Supreme Court that mandatory prayer time and Bible reading violated her son's constitutional rights.

In my opinion, it's been all downhill since then. And now? Well, according to polling done by NBC, we are at a boiling point. According to their poll published in August 2022, only 21 percent of Americans believed our nation is going in the right direction. The majority of those polled, 74 percent, had the opposite view, that America is going down a dangerous path. Even more telling is that 54 percent of the respondents felt that America's best days are behind it.[3]

People are afraid for our future. While they may not know why they are fearful, more and more people are less confident about what lies ahead. The danger of this uncertainty about our culture is that people grow desperate for leaders who will usher us into a better promised land. We want someone to step forward to lead us out of moral decay. We want solutions! We demand something better!

Unfortunately, there are any number of politicians, pundits, and celebrities who stand ready to offer us their opinions about how to restore order. All we need to do if we want what they are selling is to give them the reins and get out of the way.

There is a problem with the promises these self-appointed saviors are making. They have one thing in common with the rest of us: they are all flawed people. Some may be better qualified than others, some may even possess better character than the majority, but at the end of the day, they are all imperfect. They may have a platform and a microphone, but they aren't any smarter than we are, and their solutions aren't going to bring about real hope and change.

According to the NBC poll, most Americans think our culture is actually deteriorating. We are going backward! I am not all that confident that either the elephant or the donkey party can get us out of this mess we find ourselves in.

Israel was a nation that frequently flirted with collapse. In many ways, they suffered the same ailments we are facing right now—murder, infanticide, and sexual perversion. Every example in the Bible of Israel's national decline follows their rejection of the authority of God.

But despite their drift away from God, he was always ready to take his unruly children back. He even gave them a blueprint for getting back on track.

> If my people, which are called by my name, shall humble themselves, and pray, and seek my face, and turn from their wicked ways; then will I hear from heaven, and will forgive their sin, and will heal their land. (2 Chron. 7:14 KJV)

However, if I'm going to humble myself before him, I must have confidence in his ability to forgive me of my sin and heal me. This isn't something I can enter into half-heartedly. I need to know for sure whether or not he's powerful enough. I must also be confident of his goodness before I can make myself vulnerable to him.

So, who is he? Specifically, who is Jesus, since he is God in the flesh? What are his qualifications? Can I depend on him?

We shouldn't shy away from seeking the answers to these questions because everything depends on him being who the Bible claims he is.

Jesus, the Eternal God

When the apostle John wrote his gospel about the life of Jesus, he began his biography by making the boldest of claims.

> In the beginning was the Word, and the Word was with God, and the Word was God. He was with God in the beginning. (John 1:1–2)

There have been a lot of claims about who Jesus is. Some say he was only a prophet, while others say that he was just a good teacher. Still others claim that either he was a lunatic or a liar. And there are some who claim that he never really existed, that he was a mythological character, like Zeus or Poseidon.

People are going to have to decide for themselves who Jesus really is, but the Jesus I want to talk about is the Jesus of the Bible. He's the only one I care about.

When I first read the above passage in John 1, I thought to myself, *Who is this Word person?* As I continued to read, I found out who the Word is.

The Word became flesh and made his dwelling among us. We have
seen his glory, the glory of the one and only Son, who came from the
Father, full of grace and truth. (John 1:14)

John identifies Jesus as the Word, the ultimate authority on everything. The way I see it, if his claims are true, that he was murdered and
raised from the dead, he is the authority. If his resurrection is a historical fact, no one could seriously argue that he isn't worthy of my praise.

Resurrection defies every law of nature we know. Once something
is dead, it's dead like Rover, dead all over. There is no coming back
from that, that is unless a supreme, almighty, infinite God intervenes
and reverses the laws of science. In Jesus' case, Satan killed the earthly
body of Jesus, but by God's power, he was raised from the dead.

Not only does John claim that Jesus is eternal, with no beginning
or end, he also claims that Jesus was the one responsible for creation.

Through him all things were made; without him nothing was made
that has been made. In him was life, and that life was the light of all
mankind. (John 1:3–4)

When most of us think of creation, we imagine some distant God
speaking it all into existence. However, since Jesus' appearance in the
flesh, we now have a visual image of our Creator. He is God, but he is
also a man of skin and bones. When God came to live here, he came
eating and drinking. He is like us in this way, but he's also different
in that he is God, and as God, he is the one who made us and put air
in our lungs.

What a preposterous idea that the Creator would become one of us, walk around on this planet for thirty-three years, die a brutal death, and be raised from the dead. But that is the story John tells about him. The God who created every atom and molecule in the entire universe walked on earth as a man.

The God who created every atom and molecule in the entire universe walked on earth as a man.

But if it's true? It is the greatest story ever told. We'll talk more about the shocking humanity of this Creator God—and what his humanity means for you and for me—in the next chapter. But before we get to that, I want to draw your attention to what the wonders of creation tell us about Jesus.

Jesus, the Word of God, Is the Creator

According to the Bible, all God had to do was say, "Let it be!" (with apologies to the Beatles) and every bit of creation began to be. That's it. He spoke and it began to exist. An accomplishment like that seems like a lot of work to us, but it wasn't for God. He just said the word, and it was done. Just like that. Jesus is that Word of God, the Creator who brought all things into existence.

And what an amazing universe he created for his glory and our enjoyment. From the trillions upon trillions of celestial bodies that occupy space across the vast universe to the unseen world of atoms and the cells of living things, our environment is incredible. In fact, it is so vast and so precisely designed that the only thing we can say about it is that it is *unfathomable.*

I'm no scientist, but I've been an observer of the cosmos for over seven decades. I've seen a thing or two, even back when I was a rank and filthy sinner, that caused me to take pause for a moment and wonder to myself, *How did it all get here?*

I've discussed these things before, but I was awestruck at a young age by the annual migration of waterfowl. Even as a young boy traipsing through the woods and swamps in Northwest Louisiana, my observations led me to ask simple questions about the origin of the universe. How do ducks know when it's time to leave the far north and head south for the winter? How do they know the way? How do they find the same ancestral water holes year after year? The same flight patterns? The same migration routes? The same stops along the way?

And then there is the pesky beaver. In my persistent fight with the *Castor canadensis*, the North American beaver, I also marveled at their uncanny ability to construct intricate dams and huts out of sticks and mud. They will not, they cannot be deterred. Embedded deeply within their DNA is something that commands them to stop the flow of water, and they will not relent until they have accomplished the one task they've been designed to complete. To say they are driven to do what they do is an understatement. They are equipped to do this, either by the impersonal forces of evolution or by an all-powerful, all-knowing Creator who implanted this unquenchable desire in every cell. You decide which one you're going with. All I know is that their entire lives are spent working like crazy to impede the flow of water.

As I said, it's not just that beavers build dams and huts, but that the knowledge of how to accomplish that task seems to be implanted in their brain. The beaver comes out of his mother's womb with that particular skill set intact. I concluded early on that they are so hard-wired to do what they do that nothing mankind does will stop them. Trust me! I've tried. I hate to admit failure, but even though I may have won a battle or two, the beaver has so far won the war.

As much as I despise the destruction they cause, however, I am amazed at how well they do their job. No training! No schooling! Simply by instinct. Nothing more! In fact, I don't think it's knowledge at all. It's more like an uncontrollable impulse, like breathing or the blinking of eyelids, like they were designed by a superior being specifically to accomplish that one task.

Observing things in the woods is where I began to question why things exist. Even the most committed skeptic would be forced to admit that waterfowl migration and dam-building beavers are at least worthy of note. At the very least, almost everyone who observes the same things I see will say, "Hmm, that's interesting." Right?

As I said, I am obviously no scientist. In my early days, I coached high school sports and taught a few English classes. In my late twenties, I designed the duck call that has supported our family for almost fifty years. Sixty days or so out of every year, I rise early in the morning, take a short jaunt to one of my blinds, and there I unceremoniously harvest ducks. The rest of the year, I'm either plowing the earth and planting the crops that will feed the wildlife I will harvest or repairing and brushing duck blinds.

I'm really just a simple man living a simple life. There's not much to me, to tell the truth. So, if you were to ask me to explain the universe in scientific terms, I would have to refer you to someone more qualified.

This, however, is the beauty of creation. It so overwhelmingly declares the reality of God that we don't have to be astrophysicists or molecular biologists to marvel at creation. Even a phys-ed teacher and duck call maker can be dazzled by it.

Yes, even the simplest and most unsophisticated people can see what both the scientists and I see and be dumbfounded by its majesty. Something about creation seems to be screaming in our ears that there is more out there than we can imagine. That inaudible voice tells you and me that something or someone is behind it all, and that this creative force is amazing beyond our comprehension.

The Vastness of Creation Points to an All-Powerful Creator

I'm not the first one to make this observation. Three thousand years ago, David said, "The heavens declare the glory of God; the skies proclaim the work of his hands" (Ps. 19:1). David saw what you and I see. His eyes were focused on creation, but what he saw turned his mind to God.

The amazing thing is, David penned those words millennia before the James Webb Space Telescope was launched. The latest images sent back from space are dazzling, breathtaking. Peering deeper into space than man has ever been able to see before only confirms what we already knew: this universe is diverse and big. It is incomprehensibly vast. I see what we all see in the night sky with our naked eyes, but when I saw the Webb pictures for the first time, it left me speechless.

The only thing I could say was, "God, you really are there!"

David had no such access to technology. Still, he came to the same conclusion I did. He just looked up with his naked eyes and marveled. To him, creation was really big. We now know that it's much, much larger than David could have known. But even then he was able to determine one thing to be true: the vastness of it all was more than he could fathom. And what he saw compelled him to utter the same name that I spoke—"God!"

Yes, the universe is large. But that word *large* is a relative term. A man standing six-foot-eight-inches tall and weighing 450 pounds would be considered large when you compare him to a skinnier or shorter man.

But from the deep recesses of space, he's not much at all really. If we looked back at earth from out there, we couldn't say that he would appear larger than the smaller man, because we wouldn't have to travel too far above the earth's surface before we wouldn't be able to see him at all.

We aren't talking about that kind of big. When speaking of the size of the universe, we're way past that.

So, how big are we talking, Phil?

Once you crunch the numbers on the size of the cosmos, it almost makes the question laughable, because the answer is that no one really knows. What we do know is that the *known* universe is ninety-three billion light-years across. That's a best-guess estimate. But that's just what we know about. Scientists theorize there is more, much more. They just don't know how much more.

So, we wonder, is the universe twice the size of what we know? Three times? And what if we even could see the outer perimeter of the cosmos? What's after that? Nothing? But when you say that nothing is there, what in the world does that even mean? I can't fathom nothingness because everything I have ever known is something.

As mind-boggling as the concept of nothingness is, what if this thing just goes on forever and ever? What if there is no end to it? Can we even imagine that?

We're just getting started, and my head is already spinning! The only thing we can say is that the universe is larger than any human can grasp with his finite mind. So, to help us have a better idea of how big it all is (the part we know about), let me offer the redneck explanation for what a light-year is.

Light travels at 186,000 miles per second. By anyone's calculations, that's pretty fast. I know that rednecks are accustomed to calculating speed in miles per hour, so let me break it down for all you NASCAR fans: light travels through space at 670.6 million mph. We say that things are "lightning fast," but lightning is slow in comparison. It creeps along at only 276,000 mph. Lightning is the tortoise in the race with the hare. So when we say that the *known* universe is ninety-three billion light-years across, we are talking about a distance so vast that, even if humans could travel at the speed of light, no one human could ever complete the journey.

I also know what some of you dirt-track-racing boys are thinking: *There's gotta be a way to tweak that spaceship and make it go faster. Maybe a souped-up turbocharger would do the trick.*

Sorry, Junior. It ain't going to happen. Even if you and I could make it to the edge of the universe, and even if we could travel at the speed of light (which Einstein said is impossible), and if we traveled at that speed for an entire lifetime, we would have made almost no progress at all.[4] The distance is simply too great. More than we can imagine. Even if we could travel at 670.6 million mph, it would still take ninety-three billion years to make the journey.

All I can tell you is that you would need to pack your lunch if you set out to make a trip like that.

These are mind-blowing distances. Incomprehensible! But hold on, there's more!

After considering the sheer size of the cosmos, I wondered exactly what is out there in space. How many stars? How many planets? What I found out is that there are so many celestial bodies in the universe we can't even count them all.

Just our galaxy alone, the Milky Way, has approximately one hundred thousand million stars. But how many stars are in the universe? In total? All the best astronomers can do is make an educated guess.

The numbers are staggering. In all of the known universe there are from one million quintillion to two million quintillion stars in space.[5] I am not sure how many that really is, but I think it's one hundred to two hundred billion trillion.

This is way above my head, so let's talk about galaxies. That should make it easier, right? Would you like to hazard a guess about how many there are? A hundred? A thousand? A million? Go big! Really big! Don't be afraid of swinging for the fence here.

Opinions vary, but scientists estimate there are between two hundred billion to trillions of galaxies.[6] And that's just in the known universe.

We toss that word *trillion* around like it's nothing. Politicians do it all the time. What's a trillion dollars to a senator or a congressman? But it's a really big number, so to give you an idea of how big, let me give you an analogy.

If you were to borrow a million dollars and pay it back at the rate of one dollar per second, it would take you eleven days to repay your debt. Borrow a billion dollars and pay it back at the same rate, and you would be debt-free in around thirty years.

But, and this is where we begin to realize just how big a trillion is, if you borrowed a trillion dollars and paid it back at one dollar per second, it would take you thirty thousand years to get out of debt.

We aren't talking about one trillion galaxies, but trillions, as many as two hundred trillion.

Meanwhile, all of these galaxies, stars, and solar systems are operating methodically and rationally. They move in a sort of cosmic dance that is repeated year after year, millennium after millennium, spinning, rotating, hurtling through space in an orderly fashion that almost looks like someone organized things that way.

I will remind you again that this is exactly what David said in Psalm 19: "The heavens declare the glory of God; the skies proclaim the work of his hands" (v. 1). Once again, David came to the same conclusion that you and I have come to: God! Not a doubt in his mind or mine. Even without the technology that permits us to gaze deeper into the bowels of the universe than David ever dreamed possible, he was still able to see the heavens and skies for what they were—evidence that God is real. He knew that it is impossible for everything that exists to begin to exist if there weren't someone far superior to mankind behind it all. Someone bigger and more powerful than the human mind can comprehend.

The Harmony of Creation Points to a Divine Designer

As I've said, I have spent most of my life in the woods hunting wild game or harvesting the crown jewel of all fish from the muddy waters of the Ouachita River, the Opelousas catfish. And while it is true that I am single-minded in my focus on killing and catching wildlife for our dinner table, I also take note of the things I see along the way. Things that most people might take for granted.

Besides the beaver and the migration of waterfowl, one of those phenomena I've taken note of is the seasonal changes in plants. At my age, I've witnessed over three hundred changes of the seasons—winter, spring, summer, and fall. I understand that most folks take notice of seasonal changes and say things like, "It's getting colder, winter's on the way," and "The leaves are beginning to bud out on the trees. Spring is here." But those observations are the extent of their thinking. They see it, but they don't often wonder why or how it's all happening.

Many years ago, however, it occurred to me that changes in the vegetation that are brought on by the changing of the seasons are, in themselves, a sort of miracle. What internal mechanism signals to the tree that it's time to either sprout new vegetation or shed its existing leaves?

When I did my research on this question, I didn't get a real answer. Most of the articles I read said something like, "Trees shed their leaves in the fall because winter is coming and they can't supply the nutrients the leaves need once the days are shortened."

I said to myself, *So you're telling me that trees just happen to know when winter is approaching, when less sunlight will be available for photosynthesis, so they drop their leaves? Random evolutionary processes just equipped plants with this unique strategy to preserve the integrity of their woody core during the winter months?*

Yeah, I'm not buying it! There's just too much design in what I see for it all to have happened by chance.

Thankfully, as David said, God has left an undeniable trail of evidence that he is real. It's everywhere you look. From the heavens and the skies to the trillions of cells that make up our bodies, he has left his calling card in and on literally everything we can experience with our five senses.

Sometimes, when Miss Kay is off on one of her "vacations" and I'm all alone in my recliner down here in the middle of the woods, I think back to the day of my conception. I don't remember it of course. My cohort Skip boasts that he remembers the day of his birth, but even Skip draws the line at claiming to recall his own conception. However, I do know that there was a day, over seventy-six years ago, that one of my father's sperm cells penetrated one of my mother's eggs and one cell began to exist. Not long after, that cell was given a name: Phil Alexander Robertson.

Talk about humble beginnings, that's as humble as it gets. Just a one-celled creature imperceptible to the naked eye.

Human conception is a miracle all its own. But the rest of the story is equally compelling—how one cell becomes two cells and two become four and four become eight until, a few months later, a new human being consisting of trillions of cells bursts forth from his mother's womb, fully prepared to take his place among the rest of the Robertson brethren.

And all along the way, something (or someone) marshaled those cells to become different parts of what would become my body. Some cells went off to become my skeleton, while others formed my circulatory system. Others formed my arms and eyes. Everything about my human body began on the day of conception. One cell that became many, each of them especially designed to become the different parts of my body. Something, some force, some being directed every cell division and specialization until there I was: a slimy, crying, peeing, sucking miracle who didn't exist nine months before.

No doubt about it, I am miraculously and wonderfully made. And so are you. Our fetal development was guided by the hand of God while we were still in that "secret place." Like a weaver, God skillfully knit about twenty-six trillion cells together before we ever took our first breath of fresh air.

> I praise you because I am fearfully and
>> wonderfully made;
>> your works are wonderful,
>> I know that full well.
> My frame was not hidden from you
>> when I was made in the secret place,
>> when I was woven together in the depths of the earth.
> Your eyes saw my unformed body;
>> all the days ordained for me were written in your book
>> before one of them came to be. (Ps. 139:14–16)

Yes, everything that was needed to become you was coded into that original cell. Your skin tone, the texture and color of your hair, the color of your eyes, your body type, the shape and size of your nose—everything about your physical body and even perhaps your temperament was all prerecorded inside that cell in one DNA molecule. Scientists have studied fetal development in depth, and they have learned a lot about it, but I'm not sure they understand the mechanism that drives it.

Some may be confused about the science of it, but the Lord wasn't. He told the prophet Jeremiah, "Before I formed you in the womb I knew you" (Jer. 1:5).

The miracle of birth and human development has the stamp of the Almighty all over it, and Jesus was right in the middle of it, directing it all. Before any of us made our appearance on Planet Earth, God not only knew us, but he planned to form us cell by cell until we were fully developed.

Somehow, "it just happened" doesn't seem to do the trick for most of us.

I've already confessed that I am no scientist. However, I am fully capable of seeing the created universe for what it is. From the vastness of the cosmos to the minutiae of the microscopic, to the miracle of conception and fetal development, I see design everywhere I look.

There's no doubt about it in my mind—someone's in charge of this thing, someone who is far greater than any human being we have known. His majesty and his glory revealed in creation leave no doubt that he's the only true God with unimaginable creative power.

Why Jesus' Identity as the Creator Matters

You may be asking, *What's the big deal? Why does all of this creation stuff matter?*

As it turns out, there isn't one single question you could ask about Jesus that is more important than that. It all boils down to this: If Jesus' claims about himself are accurate, beginning with his creation of everything, then there is no one else we could go to in order to find out what our purpose for being here is. He alone has the authority to define reality for us. All of our confusion about everything can be cleared up when we see his mighty power displayed in creation. Trillions of celestial bodies are crying out in unison across the universe, "He alone is God!" All of life is crying out, "He alone is the sovereign God!" Every atom and molecule from one end of the universe to the other are making the same cry: "He is God!"

If this is true, we can bank on one fact. When Jesus said "All authority in heaven and on earth has been given to me" (Matt. 28:18), we can be sure that he spoke the truth. We can trust him. We can take him at his word.

Jesus, as the agent of creation, is reliable. He is never ambiguous or confusing. And he never steers us in the wrong direction. I can follow his every step, trust his every word, and believe his every claim about himself and about me.

In heaven, where he sits at the right hand of the Father, the angels worship him in unison:

Day and night they never stop saying:

"'Holy, holy, holy
is the Lord God Almighty,'
who was, and is, and is to come." (Rev. 4:8)

When the multitudes in Revelation 5 collided with the Creator, they were forced to cry out:

"Worthy is the Lamb, who was slain,
to receive power and wealth and
wisdom and strength
and honor and glory and praise!" (v. 12)

Jesus, as the agent of creation, is reliable. He is never ambiguous or confusing.

Anytime anyone in the Bible ever had an encounter with the crucified and risen Lord Jesus, they praised him:

"To him who sits on the throne and to the Lamb
be praise and honor and glory and power,
for ever and ever!" (Rev. 5:13)

In answer to the question about why this matters, this is it. Jesus chose to become a lamb, one who willingly sacrificed himself for all of us. But, at his resurrection and ascension back to the Father, he became a fierce lion. Lambs are gentle creatures, bred to be slaughtered. But lions? Well, that's another matter altogether. You don't mess around with lions. Ever!

The following passage from C. S. Lewis's *The Lion, the Witch, and the Wardrobe* captured the postresurrection persona of Jesus in the character of Aslan:

"Aslan is a lion—the Lion, the great Lion."

"Ooh" said Susan, "I'd thought he was a man. Is he—quite safe? I shall feel rather nervous about meeting a lion." . . .

"Safe?" said Mr Beaver . . . . Who said anything about safe? 'Course he isn't safe. But he's good. He's the King, I tell you."[7]

Because this lion is the Creator of the cosmos, he is not a being to be trifled with. We should know that so we don't fall into the deadly trap of trying to kick him off of his throne. God is God! We are not! And any attempt to be our own god is doomed to fail. We just aren't up to the task.

What's more important, however, is that we need to know of his power and worthiness if we are going to trust him with our lives. Only a star-breathing god is qualified to be my God. Nothing less will do.

As we unpack this thought in the following chapters, you should know that this is the foundation of everything I am trying to say. God is supreme! He is sovereign! And because Jesus is the agent of creation, of everything that exists, because he created me, he has full authority over me, whether I recognize that or not. And the only way I can escape the feeling that I am so small that I don't matter is to discover the overwhelming love that this holy, righteous, majestic, universe-creating God has for me.

If I am going to follow him, if I'm going to surrender control of my life to him, I need to understand how big he is and how small I am in comparison to him. Knowing that his majesty and glory are incomprehensible to me is what makes his invitation to enter his presence and enjoy his beauty so appealing.

Yes! A star-breathing God who focuses all of his affection on you and me is the story I will tell here.

two

JESUS, THE KING OF KINGS

What Jesus did here in Cana of Galilee was the first of the signs through which he revealed his glory; and his disciples believed in him.

JOHN 2:11

For all the beauty and magnificence of creation, we also know it's a pretty messed-up place. Just take a look at some of the headlines I've noticed while writing this book:

- "Fentanyl Helps Push Overdose Deaths to Record Level in New York City"[1]
- "Suicide Rates Resume US Rise After Two Years of Decline, CDC Report Says"[2]
- "Ukraine War: US Estimates 200,000 Military Casualties on All Sides"[3]

- "Violent Crime in the U.S. Is Surging. But We Know What to Do About It"[4]

Those are some nasty headlines, aren't they? I don't know quite what to make of them, but to me, they look like the symptoms of a culture in decline. We seem to be heading down a very slippery slope that ends at the edge of a cliff.

But is this anything new?

A World in Decline

If you don't know much about history, or if you don't have a multidecade perspective, you might be tempted to think things were fundamentally different back in the "good old days." We were good then, right?

The truth is that America has never been completely good. Throughout the entire American narrative, if it is told truthfully, we have to admit we have always had plenty of injustice and violence. Just how bad was it "back in the day"? Well, between 1861 and 1865, roughly 620,000 Americans were killed by their fellow countrymen in the Civil War. That amounts to 2 percent of the entire population of the United States at the time being slaughtered on the battlefield. To put that into perspective for us, if 2 percent of the current population were to be killed in battle today, we would be looking at approximately six million Americans. That's a lot of death.

In the early days of our nation's history, entire populations were either exterminated by the US government or sent to internment camps. Beginning in 1830, President Andrew Jackson's administration forced the Cherokee people to surrender all of their land east of the Mississippi River and make the long, perilous journey to the territory now known as Oklahoma. During this forced migration, dubbed the Trail of Tears, some have estimated that four thousand of the fifteen thousand human beings who made this trek died of starvation, disease, and exhaustion along the way.[5]

But we don't have to go that far back in history to find examples of America's sins. Until the 1950s and '60s, large groups of American citizens were turned away from the voting polls. African Americans were routinely prevented from living in the neighborhoods of their choosing, and they were barred from the best colleges, universities, and jobs, based solely on the color of their skin.

You would think that after all the stops and starts in this grand experiment in "liberty and justice for all," we would have figured it out by now. I'm grateful for the wisdom of our Founding Fathers who at least had an ideal model in mind for how good societies and governments should operate, but we aren't there yet. We most certainly have a lot of work to do.

We still haven't learned our lesson. America is still playing the injustice game.

Since 1973, when *Roe v. Wade* was codified as law, over sixty-three million babies have had their innocent lives snuffed out in America's abortion clinics.[6] I have made it clear that I'm trying to stay away from politics, but this isn't a political issue any more than Christian opposition to slavery, the genocide of Native Americans, or Jim Crow laws were political.

Since *Roe v. Wade* was overturned by the Supreme Court in June 2022, many states have passed legislation that makes abortions more difficult to get. I am grateful for this kind of moral leadership. However, as long as abortion on demand is available anywhere, it means that we still have a ways to go before we can seriously claim to be a just and righteous society. In my opinion, just and righteous nations don't murder their children.

Sadly, we have always had our share of wrongdoing in America. If you want to be nostalgic about the past, you would have to ignore its painfully sordid history. If you are hopeful about the future, you would have to ignore mankind's tendency to do the wrong thing. Either way, no matter how nostalgic or hopeful we are and despite our best intentions, we just can't seem to get it together.

So, what are you saying, Phil? Should we just throw in the towel? Hardly! That's not how I live. I don't care what evil is going on around me, I'm not giving up. While I mourn the carnage that sin unleashes, I still live with an incredible hope for my future. I have said that I'm *Happy! Happy! Happy!* but the truth is, I'm more than happy. I am filled with an incredible joy that can't be described.

> Though you have not seen him, you love him; and even though you do not see him now, you believe in him and are filled with an inexpressible and glorious joy, for you are receiving the end result of your faith, the salvation of your souls. (1 Peter 1:8–9)

I haven't seen Jesus, but I do love him. Not only that, I believe in him. As a result, I am not destroyed or even disheartened because of what goes on around me. Why would a man who is being given this invaluable salvation from condemnation, sin, and shame turn around and despair over an imploding culture?

He wouldn't!

The reality is that our culture is deteriorating, but so is the entire cosmos. The whole thing is going to burn down one day (2 Peter 3:10). Yet, despite the deterioration of every physical thing, those who have put their hope in the resurrection of Jesus don't have to live in fear. Because of our faith in Jesus, we are good to go, no matter what happens.

Different Expectations

What I am saying is that we must have different expectations.

I don't remember the year, but it was somewhere in the mid-to-late 1960s. Late in the fall semester, I received a call from the man who managed married housing at Louisiana Tech. He informed me that the dean of men would like a conference with me.

It's been a while since I was enrolled at any university, so I have no idea if they even have a dean of men at LA Tech today. In case you are unfamiliar with the position, he was what you might call the policeman of the male students. His job was to make certain that young college boys didn't have young ladies in their dorm rooms and that they weren't consuming too much alcohol.

But I was in married housing, so I figured that, since I was a football star, he wanted to give me some kind of award. Imagine my shock when I found out that what he really wanted to give me was a good old-fashioned butt chewing.

He leaned back in his swanky leather office chair, looked down his nose condescendingly, and asked me a question he already knew the answer to: "Mr. Robertson, what street do you live on?"

I stammered a bit and replied, "Uh, that would be Scholar Drive, sir."

He elevated his nose a bit more and hammered out his next sentence syllable by syllable, as if trying to ensure that I would not misunderstand.

"Mr. Robertson, I don't know how to tell you this, but you aren't a very scholarly person in my opinion."

Ouch! That hit me like a ton of bricks. I mean, I wasn't valedictorian material, but my grades weren't that bad.

He continued, "The president of this fine university entertained a group of potential donors yesterday and thought that it would be helpful to show them our new married housing apartment complex. Imagine his embarrassment when they passed by your apartment."

He paused for a moment as if waiting for me to fill in the blanks. The problem was, I had no idea what he was talking about.

"Look, Mr. Robertson, boats, motors, decoys, fishing nets, and deer carcasses don't look very scholarly, especially when the president is trying to raise money for the school. Do you understand what I'm trying to tell you?"

I didn't understand. In fact, I was stunned. I had no idea what the problem was. The Robertsons didn't spend a lot of time on lawn maintenance, if you know what I mean. In our opinion, the yard was where you placed valuable stuff that you might need later on for harvesting game and fish. It was a good place to keep it.

Apparently, the good dean and the president of the university didn't share my sentiments. I hesitated for a moment or two before gruffly asking him, "What do you want me to do about it?"

He sat upright and his voice became forceful. "Clean it up!"

Clean it up? What did he think I was supposed to do with it?

"What are you talking about? That's my hunting and fishing stuff. I can't just clean it up."

Louisiana Tech's dean of men and the president of that fine academic institution had me pegged: "That Robertson dude is no scholar, and he's unworthy of representing our college."

Fast-forward to the year 2013. *Duck Dynasty* was in full swing, and I couldn't walk into a convenience store without being inundated with requests from rednecks for my autograph. I came into the house after a long day of filming, and one of the ladies Miss Kay hired to take care of the chores that accumulated during filming said, "Phil, the president of Louisiana Tech called, and he wants you to call him back."

My first thought was, *Are they still griping about the mess I had in my yard while I was living on campus? They need to let that go!*

I finally got around to calling him, and what he told me was the shock of all shocks.

"Yes, Mr. Robertson, it's such an honor to talk to you! We have inducted two former student athletes into the Louisiana Tech University Hall of Fame, and you and Terry Bradshaw are the winners. We would like to honor you both at halftime during the game with Tulane, and we would be pleased to have you in attendance."

After all those years had passed, I was to be honored for my scholarly achievements? How ironic! To be honest, I was kind of proud of being selected until old Bradshaw laughed and informed me of the real reason they wanted to honor me. It turns out they thought I was rich and expected a large donation from me. Talk about taking the wind out of my sails.

Still, I attended the festivities and stood by as they unveiled a large plaque with my likeness and name on it. Each recipient had the privilege of selecting a short statement that would be engraved on the bottom of the award. Mine says, "Phil Robertson, follower of Jesus."

I thought about their expectations of me in the 1960s. Truthfully, I was just another piece of meat to them. A quarterback who could throw a tight spiral and score touchdowns. People would attend Louisiana Tech's football games, in part, to see me toss around a piece of pigskin. If not for that talent, they would have never known who I was.

What they couldn't have known all those years ago is that the very thing that looked unscholarly to them is the very thing God would later use to propel me into my limited time in the spotlight. As it turns out, I had one talent long before I ever met Christ—hunting ducks. And he used that one talent to use me to preach the gospel.

I don't think God is impressed with my ability to harvest ducks or catch fish. I mean, he created both species, for crying out loud, so why would he marvel when I reach my limit of dead mallards? But he did see something in me when no one else did. Long before my sister Janice Ellen went after my soul with unrivaled passion, God already knew what he was going to do with me.

The problem was, I didn't know it, and the university sure didn't know it. All they saw was the mess in my yard. What they *didn't* see was how the Almighty would put me before millions to speak his name, and he would use the very thing they almost ran me out of married housing over to get the job done.

I don't hold it against the dean of men or the president of the university. They were as clueless as I was.

I often wonder what would have become of my life had I taken a more traditional life path. What if I had studied accounting and spent the next fifty years doing tax returns for rich farmers and oilmen? Would God have used me in the same way?

I doubt it! Not that I don't appreciate tax accountants who keep me out of trouble with the IRS. But in retrospect, I am happy that God has used my unique gifts of hunting and storytelling to tell folks about Jesus.

God had a plan for me in the aftermath of my college days that no one else could have seen coming. God, and God alone, knows what will fulfill us, what will give us peace of mind. And he knows that what we believe about who is really in charge of the universe is the beginning of living our best lives. If I had continued to believe that I was responsible for determining the present and the future, I would have spent all the intervening years living an anxious life with no joy and no purpose.

I thank him that he finally got my attention.

Kingdoms Without the King of Kings

I've mentioned this before, but just look at all of the dynasties and kingdoms founded on human wisdom and ruled by humans that are scattered throughout history. They all eventually collapse. In the case of some empires, like Greece and Rome, modern countries or cities bearing their names still exist, but they are only dim reflections of their former glory. Others have disappeared altogether. And as hard as this is to say or hear, the United States of America will collapse too. Personally, I hope that it's long after I'm gone.

This may sound like bad news, but if you are a follower of Jesus, you have good news to share with a world that seems to be continually disappointed in the failure of human systems. In order to be liberated from our addiction to these things, we must first accept one cold, hard fact: *there are no utopias.* Paradise in this life is a myth. If a perfect culture is your goal, you will be disappointed because no culture, no country, no society, no church is ever perfect. All of them will let you down.

> *If a perfect culture is your goal, you will be disappointed because no culture, no country, no society, no church is ever perfect.*

The good news is there is evidence in history and in Scripture that there is a better kingdom that really is *a more perfect union.* In fact, God's promise is that this kingdom is not just *more perfect* but that it *is* perfect in every sense of the word. This isn't just a fuzzy idea that we can strive for but never attain. If Jesus' claims about himself are true, we can count on this kingdom. The day is coming when human governments will be eliminated and the kingdom of God will be the only one left standing. But we don't have to wait until then before we can begin to enjoy the benefits of citizenship in the kingdom of God. We can do that now!

The reason the promised kingdom is perfect has nothing to do with its citizenry. Instead, it is the fact that a perfect king sits on the throne of this government, and all of his judgments are good and without fault. This is the only reason this kingdom is flawless.

As I said, this is a hopeful message, especially for anyone who is completely disillusioned by what they see unfolding in culture today. We may be "tormented" in our souls, as Lot was when he saw and heard the "lawless deeds" of his culture (2 Peter 2:8). I hope you will remember that the culture of Rome was far more broken than ours. Yet, in the midst of legal infanticide and the oppressive Roman army's bootheel on the Jewish people, Paul still wrote the following:

> We also glory in our sufferings, because we know that suffering produces perseverance; perseverance, character; and character, hope. And hope does not put us to shame, because God's love has been poured out into our hearts through the Holy Spirit, who has been given to us. (Rom. 5:3–5)

So, you see, God's promise isn't that we will be filled with an inexpressible and glorious joy (1 Peter 1:8) only *after* we spend a lifetime gritting our teeth and grinding it out. This promise of hope is actually good for the present because the King of kings has poured his love out into our hearts through the Holy Spirit. When he does that, we can live joyfully right in the middle of a vile, broken, and morally bankrupt society. And while we mourn the spiritual carnage that is reflected in our headlines, we know we are good to go no matter what happens.

Before we can rest easy in the brokenness of a sin-cursed world, however, it might be good to understand how we got here in the first place. Not only that, it would also be helpful to know whether or not God has a plan to get us out of this mess.

Paradise Lost

We were created by God to live in a paradise-like environment with no pollution, crime, sin, disease, or death. As far as real estate goes, it was a prime piece of property. As I'm told they say in the business, it's all about the three most important things to consider when looking for property—location, location, location.

Think about it, our ancestors were allowed to live in a struggle-free environment with a bountiful supply of fresh and delicious food, and they didn't have to break a sweat to enjoy any of it. No job! No mortgage payments! No car repairs! In fact, though they were tasked with ruling the animals and stewarding the beautiful garden God had prepared for them, their responsibilities were a joy, not a burden. In that sinless world, Adam and Eve lived in perfect harmony with creation, and they spent their time enjoying one another and the God who walked with them in the late afternoons.

The only problem was, they blew it by listening to the evil voice that suggested they could displace God as king of the universe. And when they took a bite out of the forbidden fruit because of Satan's lie, the nature of the world changed. With one bite, sin not only entered the hearts of the first humans, but it infected all of creation and destroyed paradise.

Our problem since the garden is that we now live in a world that is cursed. We lost paradise. All of the headlines I mentioned at the beginning of this chapter are the consequences of losing paradise. This is what Paul argued when he said, when Adam sinned, sin entered the world. Adam's sin brought death, so death spread to everyone, for everyone sinned (Rom. 5:12).

When sin was ushered in, it dragged death along with it. But a laundry list of other painful ailments were also a part of the package. Because of our tendency to disregard the wisdom and authority of our Creator, our lives are characterized by the pain of a future hope that is just beyond our reach. It's painful because God put eternity in our hearts (Eccl. 3:11), but since the fall, death is our reality. We long for what we were created to have, but sin stands in the way. It hurts. Badly.

The reason the introduction of sin into the world continues to have such devastating consequences is that sin fractures our relationship with God. It tends to make us run from God. What first looked appealing to Adam and Eve soured as soon as they took one bite. Sin caused them to do what is irrational: they hid from the Creator in the bushes and tried to cover their nakedness with fig leaves.

We laugh about the stupidity of Adam and Eve trying to conceal themselves from the God who made them, but I suggest we shouldn't be too hasty in doing that. After all these years, mankind is still at it, still running from God by filling the gaps in our lives with distractions like drunkenness, drugs, sex, and materialism. All of it is our own version of Adam and Eve's fig-leaf strategy. We're just trying to hide our nakedness.

Losing paradise is like when we lose anything important. When four of my siblings and my parents died, I lost something profound. Even though I am fully aware of the fact that I'll never see them again in this life, I still have a gnawing desire to return to the days when we were all gathered around the table and told tall tales about our hunting exploits. Something in me wants to go back to that time.

Not everyone's aware that the paradise described in Genesis even existed, but every human being I've ever known has an inner desire for something better than the here and now. We may be unaware that our desire is connected to what we lost, but we know something is missing. We may also be unconscious of God's promise to our ancestors that they could live forever, but something in us fights death like it's unnatural.

We all long to return to Eden!

The mistake we have made since the garden is that, rather than do the logical thing and turn to God as the one who can restore Eden for us, we snatch the first fig leaves we see. Logically, we know they will never cover us, but in our minds, it's better than nothing.

An example of what I'm talking about is sex. God designed sex to be enjoyed by one man and one woman for life.

> "This is now bone of my bones
> and flesh of my flesh;
> she shall be called 'woman,'
> for she was taken out of man."

> That is why a man leaves his father and mother and is united to his wife, and they become one flesh. (Gen. 2:23–24)

His purpose in giving us sex was not so that we could just gratify some evolutionary instinct to preserve our DNA. (What a cynical view that is of the beauty of sex!) Sex is a gift from the Almighty that allows us to connect with that one person in a physical, emotional, and spiritual way that is unlike any other relationship. Godly sex is more than an act; it's an anchor to something more permanent. And as good as the permanent physical connection to that one person is, the story about sex gets even better. God gave us this gift to teach us about the unity between him and us, his church.

In God's mind, sex is marriage and marriage is sex. So when Paul said that a man should love his wife "just as Christ loved the church" (Eph. 5:25), he was talking about a husband whose unity with his bride is so perfect it's like they are one person. But instead of enjoying what God created the way that God created us to enjoy it, we've perverted his design.

That's just one example. When paradise was lost, the beauty of creation was warped and distorted, along with God's beautiful design for how we can live lives in a way that completely fulfills us. We traded paradise for a host of counterfeits that leave us dissatisfied and disappointed.

Paradise Restored

When you stand back and look at our track record, it would be easy to walk away from it and say, "It's all hopeless! We've blown it, and what we have lost is irretrievable!"

37

This would be true if not for one thing. The same God who was offended by Adam's sin (and ours too) has given us a book that contains one single promise that is repeated over and over again, beginning in Genesis and ending in Revelation.

After Satan deceived Adam, God threatened him with annihilation. Satan may not have fully understood what God was telling him, and he may have doubted that God had the power to carry it out. But afterward, there was no mistake God had followed through on this threat. He told Satan:

> "And I will put hostility between you and the woman
> and between your offspring and her offspring;
> he will strike your head,
> and you will strike his heel." (Gen. 3:15 NET)

This is the first hint of a future king who would strike the head of the Evil One and restore order to the chaos that was ushered in when paradise was lost. When Satan orchestrated the brutal murder of Jesus, it was, for all appearances, the end of God's Messiah. Satan had Jesus right where he wanted him, hanging on a cross, for crying out loud. End of story!

In one sense, it was the worst day in human history. The Creator receiving the death penalty at the hands of his creation? Without a doubt, this was bad news.

But it was also the best day in human history because, by killing Jesus, Satan inadvertently accomplished what he never intended to accomplish. When Jesus died, man's sin was erased. And when God raised Jesus from the tomb, no one who saw his resurrected body had any doubt that God had the power to forgive sins.

This was the last thing Satan wanted.

As it turns out, Satan had only bruised the heel of the Son of God. Three days after the devil's "victory," God crushed his head when the one the devil killed was raised from the grave.

You want to talk about a head-crushing blow? It was a head stomping like no other. God just put Satan's head under his mighty heel and pressed down. It was the beginning of the end for Satan. And while it's true he still has some power and is still on the loose, his day is coming when the King of kings will finally destroy him and his influence over us.

> And the devil that deceived them was cast into the lake of fire and brimstone, where the beast and the false prophet are, and shall be tormented day and night for ever and ever. (Rev. 20:10 KJV)

Living Victoriously in Spite of the Headlines

From time to time, I hear an athlete or some other public figure quote Philippians 4:13 just after accomplishing something newsworthy: "I can do all this through him who gives me strength."

Prosperity preachers love this verse. And to be honest, when you take it out of its context, it looks like God is promising me football victories or Grammy Awards. And what an appealing view of God, that he will empower me to "reach my most authentic self" or "realize my wildest dreams."

But this is why context is so important when reading the Bible. Look at the preceding verses:

> I have learned to be content whatever the circumstances. I know what it is to be in need, and I know what it is to have plenty. I have learned the secret of being content in any and every situation, whether well fed or hungry, whether living in plenty or in want. I can do all this through him who gives me strength. (Phil. 4:11–13)

Rather than a prosperity "You can do whatever you set your mind to" kind of gospel, it is quite the opposite. Doing "all things" is very limited in scope. What Paul actually said was that he could do the impossible: living in contentment in spite of his circumstances.

Just look at the perils he faced: hunger, physical need, and poverty. None of those things affected his joy at all. In fact, he said he was content regardless of the circumstances.

My first question when I read this for the first time was, *How can that be?* I asked that question because everything I had learned about life up to that point was rooted in my desire to consume things. Like most Americans, I had fully embraced the philosophy that says, "The more you have, the happier you are."

I believed that to be true—in spite of the fact that I'd seen plenty of unhappy rich people in my time! Just think about all the examples of celebrities who seem to possess everything but still wind up dying in despair. People like Jimi Hendrix, Janis Joplin, Michael Jackson, Tom Petty, and Prince all wound up dead after overmedicating their pain with drugs. They had it all, but it just wasn't enough.

In answer to my question—*How could this be?*—I think I'm on to Paul's secret. In the beginning of this passage, he encouraged his Philippian brothers and sisters to "stand firm in the Lord" (4:1).

In this one commandment we find his secret sauce: where we stand and who we stand with make all the difference in the world. If I stand in the public square with people who have a flawed and fatal view of what is important, I will not be able to be content in all circumstances. The same is true if I'm a loner who relies on my own limited understanding.

Where we stand and who we stand with make all the difference in the world.

I'll say this more than once, but this is my theme in this book. When I cast my eyes and thoughts on Jesus (Heb. 3:1, 12:2), it isn't long before I begin to find him beautiful. And the more beautiful he becomes to me, the more I desire him. And the more I desire him, the less I am obsessed with the fleeting things of this world.

As the old hymn says,

> *Turn your eyes upon Jesus,*
> *Look full in His wonderful face,*
> *And the things of earth will grow strangely dim,*
> *In the light of His glory and grace.*[7]

The King of Kings

I'm not in search of some reboot of Jesus. I want the real one. I don't want the one who is manageable or compliant with my desires. I want the one who began to reveal himself to his followers in the second chapter of John's gospel. I want the one who came full of both grace and truth.

The apostle John wrote that, after performing his first miracle, Jesus' disciples began to get glimpses of his glory:

> What Jesus did here in Cana of Galilee was the first of the signs through which he revealed his glory; and his disciples believed in him. (John 2:11)

When you take the story of Jesus (God in the flesh) as a whole, you begin to see a being so glorious you will become completely confident that he can take care of you. I mean, he can do a thorough job of providing for you in spite of what your circumstances may say otherwise.

Yes, the headlines are bad. Yes, the economy may be in serious trouble. Yes, you may have lost your job. Yes, bad characters may be out to get you—maybe even because you have decided to focus your whole life on Jesus, the one who died for you and was raised from the dead on your behalf. But at the end of the day, after all the circumstances have passed and new ones have replaced them, Jesus will still be the King of kings, and he will still be at the right hand of the Father, interceding on your behalf. You'll still be good to pass through the portal of death into an eternal future that, in terms of value, far outweighs everything else.

> For our light and momentary troubles are achieving for us an eternal glory that far outweighs them all. (2 Cor. 4:17)

In my opinion, this is as good as it gets. I may suffer a little in this life, but I'm living in a way that looks forward with great anticipation to my eternal future where I meet my Savior face-to-face.

three

JESUS, THE GREATEST TEACHER

"Rabbi, we know that you are a teacher who has come from God. For no one could perform the signs you are doing if God were not with him."

JOHN 3:2

Teaching? Talk about a thankless job. Low pay! Long hours! Add to those negatives the lack of respect from students, parents, and administrators, and we're talking about a profession that is on a fast downhill slide. I don't know about where you live, but Louisiana is scrambling hard to find warm bodies to sit behind its vacant teachers' desks, and it's getting harder every day.

In 2022 alone, seven thousand teachers left Louisiana's classrooms, which was 14 percent more than the previous year. Admittedly, there may be a lot of reasons why this is happening, but it appears the Pelican State is not the only one facing teacher shortages.

I suspect several factors are driving the exodus from classrooms, but from what I can tell it's a combination of the things I mentioned above—low pay, low respect, and unrealistic expectations. So, in order to make sure that enough warm bodies are in the classroom, districts are increasingly hiring uncertified teachers to fill vacancies.

This doesn't look good for the future of public education.

I believe most teachers are good at what they do, and they do it under incredibly tough circumstances. But occasionally, we read about a teacher somewhere who falls off the deep end in a way that makes us shake our heads. As with all professions, there are a few bad apples in the barrel. Just do a Google search. You'll find headlines about teachers getting fired or arrested for all kinds of inappropriate, harmful, and even illegal behavior, including assaulting or sexually abusing students, embezzling funds from schools, and more. When teachers betray the trust people put in them, the impact is devastating.

My Stint as a Teacher

I know a thing or two about teaching. Back in the day, someone told me it would be a good idea for me to have a degree in education. So, near the end of the summer of 1964, I packed my meager belongings into a duffel bag and headed off to Louisiana Tech on a football scholarship. After graduating with my master's degree in English education, I took a job in Arkansas at Junction City High School.

Even then, I had a few teaching skills, but they were not exactly honed to perfection. The advantage I had was that I had been working on sharpening my storytelling skills since I was a young boy. I had always possessed a sixth sense about what people were interested in, and I found a way to narrate my stories in a way that allowed others to visualize the stories I was weaving. I was a natural in the classroom. My students hung on my every word.

Looking back on my short career as a teacher, I can't say I was a good teacher though. For one thing, my content did not exactly line up with the school curriculum. Stories about football, hunting, and fishing are not the same as *Hamlet* and *The Pilgrim's Progress*.

Another problem I had was that my lifestyle at the time did not support the school board's goal of placing good, healthy role models in the classroom. Some of the darkest days of my life took place while I was employed as a teacher. And trust me when I tell you this did not escape the attention of my pupils. It isn't an easy thing to hide a life like the one I lived in that tiny Arkansas town. It was the typical small Southern community where your business is everybody's business. It wasn't long before most folks in Junction City found out about what I was up to.

I pray there weren't too many of those kids who wound up imitating my hedonistic lifestyle.

My point is that it takes more than skill to be a good teacher. In fact, I would be so bold as to say the content of the curriculum is far more important than the abilities of the teacher. If it's your desire to be a good teacher, you must first have something worthwhile to teach.

The apostle Paul fully understood this. While he continued to have a reputation as an excellent teacher, he claimed his teaching had nothing to do with his style or his skills:

> When I came to you, I did not come with eloquence or human wisdom as I proclaimed to you the testimony about God. For I resolved to know nothing while I was with you except Jesus Christ and him crucified. (1 Cor. 2:1–2)

So, it wasn't his gift of gab that set him apart from other teachers. Instead, according to Paul himself, his teaching was powerful for one reason only: he had a message. His message wasn't cloaked in lofty language. He simply told the greatest story ever told over and over again—the story of the crucifixion of Jesus for the sins of all mankind and his resurrection from the dead.

In spite of Paul's shortcomings as a speaker, the impact of his message was fully felt by all who heard his preaching precisely for that reason. Whenever he spoke, he did not draw attention to himself but instead pointed to the Son of God who was lifted up on a cross. He didn't exalt himself, but he stayed low and exalted the name of Jesus. Some people heard his teaching and repented of their sins and turned to God. Others heard the same message and recoiled in furious anger. Either way, no one walked away from any of Paul's sermons untouched.

When the substance of your curriculum outweighs the skill of your teaching, that's when you know that you have arrived at being a good teacher.

Unqualified Teachers

In Jesus' day, there were more than enough men proudly walking around Jerusalem who were wearing their teacher badges. You could spot them a mile away. If you'll take my advice and read the four Gospels of Matthew, Mark, Luke, and John, you'll find out right away that Jesus didn't have much patience with these so-called professors.

> "Everything they do is done for people to see: They make their phylacteries wide and the tassels on their garments long; they love the place of honor at banquets and the most important seats in the synagogues; they love to be greeted with respect in the marketplaces and to be called 'Rabbi' by others." (Matt. 23:5–7)

Teachers? Well, they certainly had the title, but only because they had taken it upon themselves to wear it. However, if we take Jesus' brutal public rebukes of them as any indication, we can assume they weren't handpicked by God to teach, that's for sure.

According to Jesus, their primary interest was not in leading people to bow before the transcendent God in humble adoration and give him glory. Instead, time and again Jesus made the very unflattering accusation that they assumed the teacher role for one purpose only—to be recognized for their piety and their religious fervor. And how they loved to be recognized. They wore special clothing as a virtue signal that they were from the teaching class. In public, they coveted the special recognition they received.

They loved to hear people say things like, "Oh, teacher, we have a special seat just for you, right up front. Thank you for coming to the party." Nope! It wasn't about God with them, but about themselves. It was about the backstage passes and the invites to the best parties. It was this public recognition they loved most, more than being in the presence of the holy and benevolent God of mercy.

The ones who got lost in these teachers' quest for power were the masses—the poor, blind, lame, and demon possessed. The teachers didn't give a rip about that bunch. They had a kingdom to build, for crying out loud. Why would they take time away from important work to fool with the likes of them?

One example of what I'm talking about occurred when Jesus entered the temple on the Sabbath and began healing people who suffered from various ailments. One man in particular had been paralyzed for thirty-eight years. You'd think teachers speaking with God's authority would have compassion on such a poor unfortunate soul. Wouldn't men speaking for God do whatever it took to tend to the needs of a person suffering like this? Furthermore, wouldn't you assume a man of God would rejoice when this cripple was healed? You would think so, but if you did, you'd be wrong in this case. Rather than celebrating the obvious miracle and the man's liberation from his condition, the teachers recoiled with anger. Jesus had commanded the paralytic to do what the teachers thought was illegal to do on the Sabbath, and they were offended. The man's crime? He picked up his mat (after being healed) on the Sabbath and walked away.

Never mind that an undeniable miracle had just been performed. Never mind that a man who had been bedridden for over forty years was now jumping around the temple courts as if he had never been sick a day in his life. And never mind that the most logical explanation for how that occurred was that God had a hand in it.

Never mind any of that. To the teachers of the law, the only thing that mattered was that this man had violated their interpretation of the law of Moses. For that, there were no excuses and no explanations! If you violated the Sabbath law for any reason, you deserved punishment. In the minds of these teachers, the law was more important than any man, including Jesus himself.

"Who is this man instructing people to sin on the Sabbath?" they asked indignantly.

But Jesus knew something they didn't know. They were blinded by their obsession with position and authority. They weren't driven by love for God or for their fellow man. They were driven by their lust for power and authority. And while they were craving law and order, they missed the most important thing: that all of Scripture points to the coming Messiah, Jesus!

> "I have testimony weightier than that of John [the Baptist]. For the works that the Father has given me to finish—the very works that I am doing—testify that the Father has sent me. And the Father who sent me has himself testified concerning me. You have never heard his voice nor seen his form, nor does his word dwell in you, for you do not believe the one he sent. You study the Scriptures diligently because you think that in them you have eternal life. These are the very Scriptures that testify about me, yet you refuse to come to me to have life." (John 5:36–40)

Jesus pointed out the obvious: he couldn't do what he did if God were not with him! Any person in their right mind would have seen this without Jesus even having to say it. This kind of miracle is so profound, so distinct from what happens in the natural world, only the God in charge of the laws of the universe could make it happen.

Had their judgment not been so clouded by their lust for position, they would have seen it too. And if they had not been so blind and deaf, they would have also seen that Jesus was exactly who he claimed to be—the Son of the Most High God! But they missed it.

So, yes, they were teachers all right. However, when they taught the people the code of law was more important to God than the people he created, they became false teachers. They quoted book, chapter, and verse in their teaching, but they didn't teach the Word of God because they didn't see the human suffering of the masses and they didn't recognize the Messiah. They missed it all!

Perhaps if they had understood the truth that James wrote about years later, they could have saved themselves a lot of trouble:

Not many of you should become teachers, my fellow believers, because you know that we who teach will be judged more strictly. (James 3:1)

And judge them Jesus did—harshly!

The folks may have been duped by these teachers, but not Jesus. He knew their hearts, and he knew in advance they were going to be the ones who would murder him. He told the twelve disciples,

"We are going up to Jerusalem, and the Son of Man will be delivered over to the chief priests and the teachers of the law. They will condemn him to death and will hand him over to the Gentiles to be mocked and flogged and crucified. On the third day he will be raised to life!" (Matt. 20:18–19)

How ironic! Men who claimed to be God's teachers delivering the Son of God over to the godless for public flogging and crucifixion. Now that's something you wouldn't expect from men who lay claim to such a title, is it?

The Greatest Teacher of All Time

After several years of college, I had listened to more than my fair share of teachers. Some were good at what they did, others not so much. Either way, I didn't learn much of value from any of them. In spite of five or six years of higher education, I was still sliding closer and closer to the edge of hell. My problem was, even though I had earned a master's degree, I still didn't know the Master.

But I thank God that someone finally introduced me to the greatest teacher of all time. When I met Jesus, I was at the end of my rope, so I was ready to hear what he taught. Once God knocked me over my head with a celestial two-by-four, I stopped long enough to listen to the good news. I realized almost instantly that I had met someone special. I recognized the authority of his teaching and knew that in him I had a teacher who would (1) get to the root of my problem (which was a crippling problem, by the way) and (2) offer me real solutions.

Not long after I began to follow Jesus, I also realized he was unlike the religious teachers of his day. Not only that, but he wasn't anything like most of the preachers and teachers I had met up to that point, either. For one thing, the Pharisees and the teachers of the law hated Jesus. Remember, they were the ones who murdered him. But the people on the other end of the spectrum, the physically infirm and those who knew they were spiritually bankrupt? They adored him. In fact, they flocked to him by the thousands.

When I finally began to study the Bible on my own, I noticed not much had changed over the past two thousand years. The messy people who had a track record of moral failure were still not welcomed in the majority of God's houses in 1976. And the self-righteous? Well, all too often they were the ones running the show. After all those years, people were still finding a way to control religion and not show the kingdom of God to others.

I thank God for people like Pastor Bill Smith, my sister Jan, and my church family at White's Ferry Road Church in West Monroe. Bill and Jan let nothing stand in the way of making sure I came face-to-face with Jesus. Once they dragged me kicking and screaming into the church of God, the people at church welcomed me with open arms.

They all wrapped their arms around me and mentored me by teaching me the Word of God. I was ushered into the kingdom so fast and so forcefully that I didn't have time to think about seeking positions of influence and leadership. Instead, I was encouraged to go directly to the cross and meet Jesus there.

I'm not lying when I tell you I was shocked by their hospitality. They invited me into their homes, asked if they could duck hunt with me, and sat in our living room for hours on end, teaching me about the greatest teacher of all time.

I was not accustomed to this kind of community. Not long after I became a follower of Jesus, I left the church building one Sunday morning, got in our old jalopy, fired up the motor, and looked over at Miss Kay. She must have seen the puzzled look on my face because she asked, "What's wrong, Phil?"

"You aren't going to believe this. A woman just hugged me and told me that she loved me."

As I said, this was a different kind of fellowship than what I had been accustomed to. Before then, the only women, besides Miss Kay, to tell me that they loved me were the drunk women I had been chasing in the bars when I was drinking. So, when a church lady said it, I thought to myself, *These people aren't any different than the people I used to run with.* I now realize I couldn't have been more wrong, something Miss Kay was more than willing to point out to me then.

"Phil, she *does* love you! They all do! You didn't know that?"

As I grew in my faith in Christ, I also acquired a new definition for the word *love.* Before then, it had been self-serving, a word used to get what I wanted. But when the love of God poured into my heart, I realized, slowly at first, that it was anything but self-serving; it was self-sacrificing.

Meanwhile, my new family poured the Word of Christ into me so furiously, I felt I couldn't process any more of their teaching. They so thoroughly equipped me to be a disciple of Jesus that I couldn't walk away from him now even if I tried. They did such a meticulous job of teaching me to listen to the teacher, Jesus, that I will continue to listen to him until I suck in that last breath of fresh air.

When I started listening to Jesus, it began to dawn on me more and more how he was so different from many of the church people I had known. Those people had their own set of rules and regulations too, just like the teachers of the law. Their rules were different from the laws of the Pharisees, but they made God's kingdom as inaccessible to me as the Pharisees' rules did for the masses in their day. When I heard their rules, I knew I couldn't keep up.

- Don't drink!
- Don't commit adultery!
- Don't cuss or take God's name in vain!

The list of rules was much longer than that, but I already knew the rules, to be honest. In my younger days, my rule breaking haunted me so much I thought something was wrong with me. *Those church people seem to be pulling this rule-keeping thing off all right. What's the matter with me? Why can't I do it?* It was almost too late for me when I found out they weren't all that good at it either. They just did a better job of concealing their rule breaking. By the time I found this out, I had almost given up hope.

Don't get me wrong, obeying God's rules is how our faith plays out. But we don't keep the rules in order to elevate ourselves or to obligate God to love us more. We obey them because we become aware of the fact that we cannot enjoy the beauty of Christ while we also have a spirit of disobedience.

Another way of saying this is we don't obey in order to obtain God's love, but we obey because we have God's love. The teachers of the law and the Pharisees missed this.

Later, I was stunned to discover that the master teacher, Jesus, was very different from those teachers whose goal was to draw the crowds to themselves instead of the Father:

> *We don't obey in order to obtain God's love, but we obey because we have God's love.*

- "Come to me, all you who are weary and burdened, and I will give you rest. Take my yoke upon you and learn from me, for I am gentle and humble in heart, and you will find rest for your souls. For my yoke is easy and my burden is light." (Matt. 11:28–30)
- "For my Father's will is that everyone who looks to the Son and believes in him shall have eternal life, and I will raise them up at the last day." (John 6:40)
- "If you keep my commands, you will remain in my love, just as I have kept my Father's commands and remain in his love. I have told you this so that my joy may be in you and that your joy may be complete." (John 15:10–11)

I could go on and on, but hopefully you get the point. Good teaching always points to the greatest teacher. It doesn't point to theological arguments that only a few people can understand. The crowds that followed Jesus were unsophisticated and common people. Around here, we call them river rats. They hadn't been to seminary. Many of them were illiterate. Most of them were poor, and for the most part, they were marginalized, on the fringes of polite society.

So, when you read the Gospels, you'll notice Jesus didn't employ too many sophisticated words or engage in deep philosophical arguments. He pleaded with these outcasts to "come to me," "look to the Son," "obey my commands and remain in my love." Everything he taught pointed his listeners to him and drew them to him. If anyone else had called the masses to themself, it would seem arrogant to us. But since Jesus is the Son of God and the Creator of the cosmos, he was leading them to seek fulfillment in him. If his claims are true, there is nothing arrogant in anything he said or did.

New Birth, a New Life

I don't know much about childbirth. But what little I do know, I learned from watching Miss Kay. To be honest with you, I wasn't around much when the older three boys were born. So when it came time for Jep to make his grand entrance into this cold world, someone told me, "Phil, you ought to go into the delivery room with Kay when the baby comes."

Let me tell you something: I've been practicing the bloody art of cleaning game and fish my entire life. I've seen my share of animal gore. But what I witnessed in that hospital as ol' Jep burst forth from Miss Kay's loins stunned me. Childbirth ain't for sissies, I can tell you that. Even though it's been forty-five years or so since I had a front-row seat to Jep's birth, I am still in awe of womanhood.

Any human being who can expel a nine-pound human being through a canal much too small for the task has my admiration, that's for sure. Any notion I had before that day that women are weaker than men evaporated in one ten-minute segment of time.

Ladies, I take my hat off to you. Childbirth is a violent and bloody thing.

Jesus often used examples from everyday life to make his point. He compared the judgment that will come at the end of time to the gathering of livestock. By using the example of a farmer planting seeds, he explained why some people hear the good news of his coming kingdom and embrace it with great joy, while others hear the same message and reject it.

This is what made him a good teacher.

But sometimes, when he was directing his teaching at the religious leaders, he used hard-to-understand images. I've said that many of the religious leaders were evil men, but not all of them were insincere. Some of them, like Nicodemus, were on a genuine search for the truth of God. We can read about him in the third chapter of John's gospel, where we find him coming to Jesus to check him out. He just wanted to know if Jesus was for real.

"Rabbi, we know that you are a teacher who has come from God. For no one could perform the signs you are doing if God were not with him." (John 3:2)

It should have been obvious to anyone, after seeing Jesus perform the miracles he performed, that there was something unique about him, don't you think? We don't know whether the events in Jesus' life are in chronological order in John's gospel, so we also don't know what signs Nicodemus was referring to. However, when we take all of the miracles of Jesus as a whole, it is an impressive list of accomplishments that proves Jesus wasn't your average revolutionary. I mean, who could heal a man born blind if God were not with him? Could a man heal disabled people or raise the dead if he didn't have God on his side? Could he turn water into wine?

Nicodemus's assessment of Jesus' identity almost went to the core of who Jesus was, but it didn't go far enough. He was curious about Jesus, even drawn to him. But the best he could come up with at this point was to recognize there was something different about Jesus.

If he had been certain Jesus was indeed the Son of God, perhaps he wouldn't have been hiding in the shadows to keep from being detected by his fellow leaders as he went to visit Jesus. But at least he was honest enough to go and find out for himself, even if he did sneak around to do it. I'll give him that.

The funny thing about Jesus' response is that he paid no attention to Nicodemus's clumsy introduction. If I had plans to plant a church in my community, and an influential member of the establishment approached me and complimented my skill set, I would thank them. Not Jesus. He went straight to the core of his message as if Nicodemus had not uttered a word.

This is why Jesus' answer seems disconnected and disjointed. It's kind of comical, because he dismissed this powerful man, a man who almost everyone in Jerusalem would have been honored to have as a visitor. He was one of the men who people greeted respectfully in the marketplace. He got the best seats at the banquets and weddings. But Jesus seemingly blew him off with an answer unrelated to his compliment: "Very truly I tell you, no one can see the kingdom of God unless they are born again" (John 3:3).

What a very odd thing for Jesus to say in response to this Pharisee. But if you'll recall, I said I wanted a teacher who can get to the root of my problem and offer real solutions. Don't beat around the bush with me! I don't have time for that. In my opinion, that's precisely what Jesus did with Nicodemus. Nick was probably thinking about God's restoring Israel's prominence on the world stage. Maybe he dreamed of militarily defeating the much mightier Roman Empire. But Jesus wanted to talk about new birth instead.

This, my friends, gets to the heart of our relationship with God. Jesus had no interest in what the Pharisees were obsessed with. He couldn't care less about political systems and military might. If he was after that, he had the mighty angelic army of God at his disposal, for crying out loud. At the snap of his fingers, he could have incinerated the Romans into a pile of ash. All he had to do was say, "Get 'em, boys," and it would have been all over.

Instead, he chose to talk about new birth. Being born again. Becoming a new person. Jesus essentially told Nicodemus, "Here's the crux of the matter. No one can see the kingdom of God unless they are born again" (v. 3).

I can only imagine what Nicodemus was thinking. *Born again? What in the world is he talking about?* Nicodemus probably hadn't witnessed the birth of a child, but he likely had seen livestock give birth. Either way, he surely knew the mechanics of birth, given the way he responded.

"How can someone be born when they are old?" Nicodemus asked. "Surely they cannot enter a second time into their mother's womb to be born!" (v. 4)

Of course, Jesus wasn't talking about babies exiting the birth canal of their mothers for a second time. He was making a spiritual point, that entry into the kingdom begins with a sort of reboot, a new birth, becoming a new person.

All of this flew over Nicodemus's head. He had no clue what in the world Jesus meant by this mumbo jumbo. It seemed incoherent to him. But I don't blame him. It would have flown over my head too. *Born again? The way to God's kingdom is to make another journey through a woman's birth canal?*

That's a legitimate question, don't you think? The Pharisees taught that the passage through the portal to God was accomplished by obedience to the law of Moses. Just obey the rules, they said. Offer the required sacrifices and pay your tithes, and you'll make it, they said. Oh, and keep the Sabbath, they said. But above all else, they said, don't forget everything goes through us, because we are the portal keepers!

This Jesus fellow was really upsetting the Pharisees' applecart. He bypassed the leaders and took the masses straight to the throne room of God the Father. I think that's why Jesus spoke so mysteriously. He knew ahead of time that he would confuse the teachers of Israel. He knew this revolutionary teaching was so unlike what Nicodemus had been taught that it would cause him to shake his head in confusion. But how could Nicodemus ever see the beautiful simplicity of God's kingdom if he did not first become disillusioned with what he thought he knew about God?

So, Jesus just doubled down—he had a point to make:

Jesus answered, "Very truly I tell you, no one can enter the kingdom of God unless they are born of water and the Spirit. Flesh gives birth to flesh, but the Spirit gives birth to spirit. You should not be surprised at my saying, 'You must be born again.' The wind blows wherever it pleases. You hear its sound, but you cannot tell where it comes from or where it is going. So it is with everyone born of the Spirit." (vv. 5–8)

New birth! A new lease on life! A new life altogether that is accomplished by the Spirit of God! And like what I witnessed when I watched Jep make his bloody entrance into the physical world, this new birth would be accomplished by blood, too, but this time, the blood would be spilled from the body of the Son of God. Nicodemus would discover later that Jesus was talking about his own blood.

What a teacher!

The new birth is a mysterious thing, that's for sure. It produces such a radically different person that the only explanation for it is that it is supernatural. It's not a religious thing, as the Pharisees taught, but a radical change that occurs when we are in an intimate relationship with the Son of God.

A lot has changed in human culture since the day Nicodemus went to visit Jesus. But no matter how many things change, some things remain the same. As in Jesus' day, one may have trouble distinguishing between church people and those who have never been to church a day in their lives. It's an ugly thing when a man assumes the title of teacher and the only difference between him and the worst of sinners is his title.

When teachers speak without the authority of God, a lot of worldly teaching tends to find its way into the teaching of the church. And maybe it's not in the words that teachers say, but in the way they operate—just like the Pharisees:

- "If you don't look out for number one, no one else is going to do it!"
- "Get while the getting is good!"
- "No one is going to run over me without paying the price!"
- "I'm just going to follow my heart on this!"

A worldly person, whether in the church or in the world, is still a worldly person. I found out long ago that being a church member is not the same as being born again.

A born-again person? That person is very distinguishable from everyone else. Jesus compared born-again people to the wind. When the wind blows, you can feel its effects, but you don't really know where it originated or where it will end up. We only see the tree branches swaying and feel the breeze on our skin, but we don't know much about wind.

A person born of the Spirit of God is like that. You know that she is different in a good way. She is not the same as she used to be, and she's no longer the same as everyone else. You may not know why, but you do notice the change, and you suspect God has something to do with it.

Who Can Be Born Again?

This new birth, this new life doesn't just happen to us. It is reserved for only one kind of person: for the one who finally wakes up and realizes their old life is worthless. I'm not just talking about the dopeheads and alcoholics like me. New birth is an offer to everyone who finally realizes that life is futile without God. It's for the person who wakes up one day and says, "I am dead in my trespasses and sins [Eph. 2:1]! I need to start over."

Before any of us can enjoy the new life that results from the new birth, we must come to the point where *we realize everything else is futile in the end*. If this hasn't hit you yet, if you're still hoping you can make something out of yourself by your own power, you've never been born again. You may be a respectable church member, but so were the Pharisees. If you want a new life, you must first come to terms with the hopelessness of your present life.

What Jesus teaches here in the third chapter of John is foundational teaching. It is the centerpiece of his curriculum. I'm well aware of the fact that it runs counter to all human constructs that mankind spins in order to find meaningful direction for how we should live. Human teaching tells us meaning can only be found in accomplishing some worthwhile task. *Do enough! Do more! Be good! Be the best! Be kind! Be kinder!*

If you want a new life, you must first come to terms with the hopelessness of your present life.

But in our hearts, we all know we've failed miserably at all of that. I won't deny the immediate thrill of accomplishing something the rest of the world will applaud. However, if we are honest with ourselves, we would be forced to admit the season of human approval is a short one. So is everything else that mankind grabs ahold of to prove their value.

I think it's clear that human approval was part of Nicodemus's problem. As a member of the Jewish ruling council, many of his cohorts would have disapproved of his flirting with the idea that Jesus was someone worth following. As I said earlier, this is why he moved in the shadows to meet Jesus. He didn't want to be seen by his peers. He was curious, but he wasn't confident enough to openly declare his allegiance to Jesus. Not yet, anyhow.

As Israel's greatest teacher, Jesus pointed his words like a laser at the precise location of the spiritual cancer that lurked in Nicodemus's soul: *you need to become a new man, born again by the Spirit of God.*

Nicodemus had a choice to make. We all do. Either we continue to blindly follow failed worldly strategies to discover the path to God, or we desire something new, a new birth.

You can do as you please, but as for me, I'm going with Jesus, the greatest teacher of all time, the master teacher who plainly teaches us how to repair our separation from God. *We must be born again of the Spirit!*

A Demanding Teacher

I was fairly skilled at manipulating some of my teachers in high school and college. Even when I was a very young man, I had one skill few could challenge me on: I could catch fish and harvest wild game. I found out early on, one way to get on the good side of some of my teachers was to share some of my bounty with them. I soon discovered that a few slabs of Opelousas catfish and a mess of squirrels somehow favorably impacted my grades. It was my version of apple-polishing, I suppose.

Occasionally, however, I would run into a teacher who would have none of that. I could usually identify them as soon as they entered the classroom, and I would mutter to myself, "No catfish for this one! I'm going to have to actually learn something in this class."

Looking back across the years, I now realize the more demanding my teacher was, the more I learned. It was the ones who could not be bought off that taught me the most. Maybe they were the teachers who cared the most about me, after all.

At first glance, it may look like the greatest teacher of all time was also too demanding of his listeners. You know, like when he made ridiculous demands, such as:

- "Whoever wants to be my disciple must deny themselves and take up their cross and follow me." (Matt. 16:24)
- "In the same way, those of you who do not give up everything you have cannot be my disciples." (Luke 14:33)
- "Very truly I tell you, unless you eat the flesh of the Son of Man and drink his blood, you have no life in you. Whoever eats my flesh and drinks my blood has eternal life, and I will raise them up at the last day." (John 6:53–54)

That's some radical stuff. We are tempted to ask, "Can I just study a manual or something and memorize a few facts about you? Why can't I just google it?" But Jesus, because he is the Son of God and the Creator of the universe, knew how temporary everything is, from the time of our birth to the day we die. None of it matters in the end, except whether or not we are born again to live a new and meaningful life. So, he demands a full-scale, all-out assault on the temporary before we can really embrace the permanent. Anything less will leave us feeling crushed between the short term and the eternal. We all intuitively know there is not one single material thing or physical pleasure that will last throughout eternity, but we are drawn to those things anyhow. And without being born again by the Spirit, we will live in this hellish limbo until we die.

It's a miserable existence. I should know since I lived the first twenty-eight years of my life in that no-man's-land. And even though I detested every anguishing minute, I didn't know that God had offered to make me a new man. I didn't know that Jesus died for my rotten sins, or that he was raised from the dead, or that he sits at the right hand of the Father, interceding for me.

I can tell you one thing though. Hearing about the new birth was the greatest day of my life. I'm certainly thankful God opened my ears and eyes so I could hear and see him for who he is. Even though this involved taking a hard look at who I had become, finding out I could emerge from my encounter with him as a new man was well worth it.

As I said, my hat is off to Miss Kay and every other childbearing woman in the world. But being offered the free gift of new birth by the Spirit rivals even that. That's why I did not hesitate when I first heard about it. I thank God he gave me a second chance.

four

JESUS, THE LIVING WATER

*"If you knew the gift of God and who it is that
asks you for a drink, you would have asked him
and he would have given you living water."*

JOHN 4:10

T here is only one emotion in hell: unmitigated despair wrapped in abject loneliness, and I am enveloped in it."[1] These are the words of Aron Ralston, whose forearm was tragically lodged between two boulders while he was hiking alone in 2003 in Utah's Bluejohn Canyon. After five days of attempting to free his arm from the trap, he finally made the only decision he could make: he broke his arm bones and amputated the decaying limb. It was his only chance of survival.

As bad as losing a limb would be, it was Aron's description of the growing and gnawing sense of loneliness and despair that really caught my attention. If the hunger, fear, and pain weren't enough, his dwindling water supply created a thirst so intense that he drank the only liquid he could find—his own urine.

I hear people say things like, "I'm dying of thirst" after they haven't had a drink for a few hours. But few of us have experienced the kind of thirst Ralston did. I've been thirsty before, but not thirsty enough to drink my own urine.

This was a man overwhelmed by desperation. His parched throat signaled his brain that his body needed hydration soon or he would die. Before long, it became an obsession, and some inner voice screamed out to him, *Drink something! Anything!*

It is then that he made one last survey of his surroundings and remembered his urine. And he did what would have gagged him only days or hours before. He filled his container and gulped it down.

Until we've been in Aron's shoes, we shouldn't say, "I would never!" The truth is, no one knows what they will actually do until they are completely out of options, until they are overcome by an "unmitigated despair wrapped in abject loneliness." Until then, you don't really know what your limits are.

The last thing I want to do is diminish the physical and emotional pain this young man experienced in 2003. It is the kind of nightmarish, bloodcurdling story that makes us cringe at the thought of it. But the reason I'm sharing his story here is because of the many parallels between his experience and the emotional and spiritual hell where all of us have lived at one time or another. I've tried to forget the details of my former life, but I will always remember the hellhole I once lived in with vivid clarity. Try as I might, I can't shake it. Based on my experience, I would say that Aron's definition of hell is just about right—"unmitigated despair wrapped in abject loneliness."

What about that word *unmitigated*? It means absolute! Something so severe that there is little or no hope that it will improve. I suppose we could call it *rock bottom*. It is a spiritual thirst that consumes us when we've run out of options. A deep spiritual thirst!

Maybe you know what I'm talking about. In the quiet of the night, when our distractions have gone to bed, and we are left with one frightening thought: *I've tried it all, and nothing seems to work.*

In spite of our thoughts from the night before, we crawl out from under the sheets the next morning and do it all over again. Day after day. Month after month. Year after year. Reaching for the same failed liquids and trying to quench our thirst.

Another Option

Living in this kind of despair, along with the loneliness and fear that accompany it, is a special kind of hell. Jesus called it thirst and hunger, but those are just words he used to communicate the depth of our torment. In my opinion, God has created us with a thirst for more. Unfortunately, there are plenty of counterfeits around—fake water. But these fakes, these superficial substitutes, are always toxic and rancid. Our fear of missing out, of being unimportant or irrelevant, will lead us to drink from poisoned wells.

This is what I did. I drew sex, drugs, and alcohol from my well. For you it may be that you like to accumulate wealth or consume things.

Maybe Amazon is your god. We are thirsty, but we don't know why, so we drink what's available. Be honest with yourself. It never ends well, does it?

No matter what we call it, spiritual thirst is what we feel after we've tried the world's strategies for filling up what is empty inside and realized the void is still there. None of our attempts to make the hopeless feelings go away are ever successful. They always fail us, leaving us emptier than we were before.

I'm going to tell you something now that might shock you. If this describes you, then you should know that God has you right where he wants you. You are the reason he came to earth and took on human flesh. He came to fill the void in your heart. He came for those who hunger and thirst for more.

"Blessed are those who hunger and thirst for righteousness, for they will be filled." (Matt. 5:6)

I would argue that all people hunger and thirst for something better. But if what we hunger and thirst for won't stand the test of time or the elements of nature, what good would it do us if we got what we wanted? It wouldn't last, and once it's gone, we are right back to square one.

I said that God has you right where he wants you, but I am not saying that he wants you to camp out there. We can't hunger and thirst for what really matters until we give up on what doesn't. Once we get to that point, we are ready to cry out to God in our pain and ask for more of him. Stuff doesn't last and always leaves us wanting. But pinning our hopes on the infinite God who created everything fills us to the brim.

It was a comfort to me to discover years ago that God honors the pleading spirit. When we call on his name, he honors our plea.

> Everyone who calls on the name of the Lord will be saved. (Rom. 10:13)

We can't hunger and thirst for what really matters until we give up on what doesn't.

I had to come to this point of utter despair myself before I could fall down before him and call on his name. It happened on the day that I finally realized it was irrational for me to think I could "gain the whole world, yet forfeit [my] soul" (Mark 8:36). When I arrived at the intersection of hope and despair, I chose to forsake everything temporary and run to the eternal God as if my life depended on it. I chose hope!

Does Jesus Care About My Empty Heart?

If you want to know the depth of Jesus' desire to fill you up with everything good, I will repeat myself here: take a few days and read the Gospels (Matthew, Mark, Luke, and John). In those four biographies of Jesus' life and ministry, you will discover a surprising pattern. Time after time, he arranged his schedule so he could have encounters with the thirstiest people of his day. Even though you might miss this if all you know about him is the Jesus you heard about from some Christians, the real Jesus is intentional about ministering to the very people who most religious people wouldn't want to be caught dead with.

One such encounter was with a woman who good people might call a slut or a whore. Married five times, she stopped pretending and just shacked up with some dude she wasn't married to. You can find the story in the fourth chapter of John's gospel.

The story begins with Jesus sitting by a well in the heat of the day. When this woman, who was from a different region and tradition, a Samaritan, came to draw water from the well, he politely asked her for a drink. Two things we need to know at this point. For one thing, good Jews didn't speak to women in public. It was beneath them to do so. And if you were a good Jew, you certainly wouldn't acknowledge a woman as morally bankrupt as this one was.

The other thing that is important to know is that Jews also didn't have much to do with Samaritans. According to the rabbis, the Samaritans were an inferior race. In fact, they were so inferior that good Jews would go out of their way to keep from passing through the region of Samaria.

But John says that Jesus "had" to go through Samaria. Maybe I'm making too much of this word, but Jesus could have done what all of the other Jews did, that is, take the long way around the area in order to avoid it. But he didn't! There was an intentionality to Jesus' journey, as if he was on a mission to have a midday encounter with this woman who was in desperate spiritual need.

Apparently, she had grown weary of the Jewish leaders treating her with contempt, because she immediately tried to bust his chops for breaking the pharisaical rules that prohibited him from speaking with a Samaritan woman.

> "You are a Jew and I am a Samaritan woman. How can you ask me for a drink?" (John 4:9)

Christians who've grown up in an era that values cultural sensitivity would have probably apologetically answered her with something like, "Oh, no! I'm not prejudiced against Samaritans. Some of my best friends come from Samaria."

But as Jesus did with Nicodemus, he didn't take the bait. He knew her thirst did not come from being marginalized by the Jewish leaders. Her need was greater than that. So, he went straight to the heart of the matter. Like a laser, he pointed his kindness at her illness. This woman was thirsty for something more than water.

> "If you knew the gift of God and who it is that asks you for a drink, you would have asked him and he would have given you living water." (v. 10)

I say that he got to the heart of the matter because, even though it was inconvenient for her to make the daily trek to get water for her family, that wasn't her primary need. She may have been physically thirsty, but her greatest thirst was for the living water of life that only God could give her. Only she didn't know that's what she thirsted for. She thought it was something else. So she drank the rancid water of sexual impurity. She flitted from one man to another, hoping that this time it would be good, or if not good, better.

John doesn't tell us what was in her head when she ran into Jesus, but based on our own experience with spiritual hunger and thirst, we can make an educated guess. Maybe she had made so many mistakes that she figured she was beyond redemption. Perhaps she heard that inner voice say, *You've done it now! You are too far gone! God will never take you back!*

You and I know that doing the same foolish things over and over and hoping for something better is insane. But she didn't know that. How could she? She was living in unmitigated despair. She figured the solution to her abject loneliness was to dump the dude she was with and find a better man who could fulfill her.

We know, because we have read the Bible a time or two, that going back to failed strategies is bound to fail. It is so irrational that Solomon compared it to a dog eating his own vomit (Prov. 26:11). I hope you don't find the analogy too impolite. But if you do, don't blame me; I'm just quoting Scripture.

But sin (drinking rancid water) is disgusting, and there is no way to get around that. As I'll bring up over and over, the point is not that we have violated some external code of law, but that we have chosen life outside of a relationship with the God of the universe. That kind of life will leave us wanting for more and never satisfying us.

We need something else, someone else!

Fortunately for this woman, Jesus put her on his calendar. She could not have known in advance that Jesus was on a mission to meet her. How could she know that she was face-to-face with the Son of God, who lived by the words, "'I desire mercy, not sacrifice. For I have not come to call the righteous, but sinners'" (Matt. 9:13)?

If you miss the radical nature of this encounter, you miss everything. A holy and infinite God who plunges into the darkness of a sin-cursed world to find sinners? A God who values mercy more than man's sacrifice? What a crazy idea!

But this is the picture of Jesus that the Gospels paint.

I don't know for sure what this lady was thinking after Jesus dropped this bombshell about living water in her lap, but I'm sure she wondered, *Who is this strange man? What's all this talk about living water?* If she was bewildered, I don't blame her; I would have been baffled too. Without a spiritual mind, it would have seemed like nonsense.

Jesus could have miraculously filled her water jugs. Indeed, he could have spoken the word and her jars would have stayed full for the rest of her life. But her thirst was deeper than the water from that well could ever quench.

Instead, he offered her not only living water, but an endless supply of it to boot.

> "Everyone who drinks this water will be thirsty again, but whoever drinks the water I give them will never thirst. Indeed, the water I give them will become in them a spring of water welling up to eternal life." (John 4:13–14)

There are a lot of things that are crucial for our survival. Water is one of them. We also need food and light. It is interesting to me how Jesus often used those areas of basic needs and pointed to himself as the ultimate fulfillment of them. "I am the bread of life" (John 6:35). "I am the way" (John 14:6). "I am the light of the world" (John 8:12). This also isn't the only instance of his claim to be the water of life.

> "Let anyone who is thirsty come to me and drink. Whoever believes in me, as Scripture has said, rivers of living water will flow from within them." (John 7:37–38)

Living Water in a Dry and Dusty Culture

I gave up my addiction to the news a couple of years ago. The reason I did so is that I found myself getting dragged into the street fights that politics has become. The news is no longer the news, but rather a twenty-four-hour cycle of negativity. If the talking heads aren't ripping public figures to shreds, they are pointing out every single flaw (as they see them) in our culture. They peddle fear!

This wouldn't be so bad if they could offer a sustainable solution. But my observation has been that the only solutions they propose are the ones that direct us to one political extreme or the other. I have long suspected, however, that most of them really have only one true objective: more than anything else, they are interested in ratings, because higher ratings equal higher profits. And what draws more viewers than fear?

Too cynical? Maybe, but I'm certain about two things when it comes to the news. One is that their solutions are often knee-jerk, quick-fix solutions that won't work. The other thing I'm certain of is that we don't even need these networks to tell us that we are sliding into a moral and spiritual cesspool. I don't care which side of the ideological or political spectrum a person is on, we are all in agreement on two things: we are one whacked-up society, and it's getting worse.

As bad as we think culture is today, however, it might have been worse in first-century Judea. And for some reason, that is the very specific culture the Father intentionally chose as the one in which he would insert his Son as an embedded foreign agent. His not-so-grand appearance was no accident. According to Scripture, it happened "at just the right time" (Rom. 5:6). The question is, why? We have to admit that it seems like an unlikely place to start the church. To begin with, the culture of Judea was controlled by men who had twisted God's law to make it easier to gain control over the people. Second, Judea was under the heavy foot of the Roman Empire.

The Romans allowed the Jews to practice their religion, but the Jews had no actual political power. In fact, only thirty-seven years after the Jewish religious leaders orchestrated Jesus' murder (with authorization from the Roman governor Pontius Pilate), Jerusalem was besieged by the Roman general Titus. After five months, the city was destroyed and most of the population was either killed or carried off to be sold as slaves.[2]

No doubt about it, first-century Jerusalem was a dysfunctional culture. But one of the consequences of the Roman destruction of Jerusalem and the Jews' holy temple was that many Jewish Christians escaped capture by the Romans and took the gospel with them wherever they went.

While we are convinced that religious freedom is a God-given right and that the church thrives best when we can practice our faith "without fear of molestation" (as the old preachers used to say), history also tells us that when Satan's minions move on God's people by persecuting, imprisoning, or killing them, it almost always fans a small glowing ember into a raging fire. One prime example is what happened to Christianity after Mao Zedong assumed control of China. An estimated forty to eighty million people were killed, many of them our brothers and sisters in Christ. Beginning in 1966, Mao's Cultural Revolution ushered in a new terror as he attempted to wipe out all public religious practice in China, including Christianity. Christians were killed and imprisoned, and church buildings were destroyed.[3]

But the atheistic Mao did not know the God of creation. He didn't know the crucified and risen Lord Jesus. He was a completely materialistic man who was under the control of the Evil One. And he certainly didn't know that humanity can only really thrive when it is in community with the Almighty.

The result of Chinese persecution was that it inadvertently created an even greater thirst among the Chinese people for something more than bread and water. In one of the greatest ironies in human history, God's church in China grew from a million or less when the persecution began to anywhere from one hundred to two hundred million today.

Today, the same miraculous church growth is taking place in Iran. In fact, some studies have shown that the church is growing faster in Iran than in any other region of the world,[4] in spite of the fact that it is illegal in Iran for Muslims to convert to Christianity. Anyone who turns to Jesus is targeted for extreme persecution, including beatings, imprisonment, and even execution.

Why would the church of Christ grow so rapidly in environments where hatred for Christianity is encoded into law? Wouldn't folks be more fearful of putting their trust in Jesus as their Savior when doing so puts their lives on the line?

This would be true if being a Christian were no more meaningful than being an Amway distributor or a member of the Elks Club. No one would risk death for cleaning products or a social group! The only rationale for preaching Jesus in the face of severe opposition and the threat of imprisonment or death is that one has been gripped by the certainty that Jesus was resurrected from the dead. This is the only explanation. It was true of the apostle Paul (1 Thess. 2:1–4). It was also true of Peter and John, who were thrown in jail for their belief in the resurrection (Acts 4:1–22):

> The priests and the captain of the temple guard and the Sadducees came up to Peter and John while they were speaking to the people. They were greatly disturbed because the apostles were teaching the people, proclaiming in Jesus the resurrection of the dead. (vv. 1–2)

Had they not been confident that Jesus' resurrection from the tomb was real, a historical event, they might have recanted at the threat of imprisonment. Instead, they doubled down on their message. Peter said:

> "Know this, you and all the people of Israel: It is by the name of Jesus Christ of Nazareth, whom you crucified but whom God raised from the dead, that this man stands before you healed." (v. 10)

You might also assume that when the crowds witnessed the arrest of Peter and John they would have scattered to the four winds. Instead, the opposition they received only served to inflame the desire of the people to have what Peter and John had, namely, a confident hope in their own resurrection from the dead by the power of God.

Many who heard the message believed; so the number of men who believed grew to about five thousand. (v. 4)

Even Jesus was able to withstand the thought of his impending death because of his confidence in his own resurrection. But it was more than that for him; he also endured because of his future reward, knowing that, by suffering, he would rescue us from the grave too.

For the joy set before him he endured the cross, scorning its shame, and sat down at the right hand of the throne of God. (Heb. 12:2)

The Fear of Death Extinguished by the Living Water

Water extinguishes fire. But in our case, God isn't promising to put out every fire in our lives. After we give our lives to his care and control, we still get sick. Broken bones and car accidents still occur. And without a doubt, we will all die.

The fire that living water extinguishes is the fire fueled by our fear of death. It's the fire that burns inside us that tells us we are missing out on something. Call it hunger or call it thirst. It is that nagging awareness that we are letting our best years slip away. It is that inner voice that feels like deep longing.

The entire world is burdened by the fear of death. Every person experiences (or tries to ignore or forget) the longing for life beyond death. But while the lawlessness and hopelessness of the world torments me, it only torments me because I know that living without Christ is a special kind of thirst. And without him, it is unquenchable. With him, however, we have a limitless source of living water that will satisfy us for eternity.

> *I know that living without Christ is a special kind of thirst. And without him, it is unquenchable.*

And Here Is the Point!

We've grown so accustomed to having church our way that we can't imagine it any other way. But I challenge anyone to find the phrase *freedom of religion* in the Bible. Before you do a Google search for it, let me just warn you first—*it ain't there!*

In fact, when you study the Scriptures to find out how we should handle opposition, the Bible doesn't say anything about relying on any earthly government to protect our freedom to believe and worship the way we want. You are welcome to check me on this, but what the Bible essentially says to those facing persecution is, "Persecution is to be expected. Suck it up and preach the good news of the resurrection of the dead!"

- "Consider it pure joy, my brothers and sisters, whenever you face trials of many kinds." (James 1:2)
- "'Blessed are you when people insult you, persecute you and falsely say all kinds of evil against you because of me. Rejoice and be glad, because great is your reward in heaven.'" (Matt. 5:11–12)
- "Everyone who wants to live a godly life in Christ Jesus will be persecuted," (2 Tim. 3:12)

I could go on, but surely you get the point. I love America, and I'm grateful we have had unfettered freedom to "do church" as we see fit. But in order to have a radical kingdom impact on the world, the world needs to know that we are serious about laying down our lives for the One we believe in. They need to know that our citizenship is primarily in heaven. The world must know that we are living for the day when we stand before the Father and hear him say, "Well done, good and faithful servant! . . . Come and share your master's happiness!" (Matt. 25:21).

If you are spiritually thirsty, living in unmitigated despair and abject loneliness, this is your solution. Bow down before our holy God, confess your sins, plead for mercy, and believe he has moved you from the temporary world of disappointment into his eternal kingdom where you will never be disappointed again.

This is also the antidote to what ails the church. And if we are following Jesus, I mean *really* following him, then we are, by nature, springs of free-flowing water that will quench the thirst of a desperate world. Call a truce to the wars on social media between believers about the finer points of doctrine, theology, and church systems and get on with the business of telling thirsty people that they can drink freely from the fountain of living water for the rest of eternity. We don't have time to be petty, because too much is at stake.

five

JESUS, OUR DEFENSE ATTORNEY

*"Let any one of you who is without sin
be the first to throw a stone at her."*

JOHN 8:7

I f you have ever wondered what the Robertson childhood experience was like, maybe one day I'll give you a front-row seat to hear
that crazy story. It wasn't dull, I can tell you that! The seven of us
were basically what you would call feral, for lack of a better term. We
traipsed unsupervised through the swamps and river-bottom forests
and toted loaded shotguns and rifles and hunted something to kill that
would provide food for our large family.

You're probably wondering what kind of parents would encourage their young boys to wander all alone through the woods with powerful firearms? Uh, maybe parents like James and Merritt Robertson would, parents who were worried about how they were going to put food in the mouths of seven hungry children.

Somehow, we all made it to adulthood alive and with all our body parts fully intact.

Our rambling house sat on the outer edge of a large cotton plantation just north of Shreveport, Louisiana. It was low-lying land that must have been the perfect habitat for snakes, wildlife, and bugs, because there were plenty of them.

Ironically, the Robertson household was insect-free, not because we kept a neat yard or always swept up the crumbs we dropped around the kitchen table. Our secret sauce was way better than that. It was that healthy dose of DDT the local farmer sprayed on the cotton fields that surrounded our dwelling on three sides.

The crop duster pilot told Ma not to worry, that DDT was so safe, a human being could gulp it down like water without any side effects at all. So he did Ma a favor and left the spray valves wide open whenever he buzzed over our house.

Keep in mind that the source of our drinking water was a large cistern that collected rainwater, so every time he dusted the cotton fields, our cistern collected a fair amount of what we found out years later was poison. I have no way of knowing how many gallons of DDT my siblings and I ingested over the years, but when I look at my brother Si, I figure it must have been a lot.

Still, in spite of our poverty, my mother's mental illness, and the large quantities of gene-altering insecticide we freely drank, there was something about the way we lived that still has a special appeal to me. I don't like to think of myself as nostalgic, but maybe I am. Times were hard, but I do have some good memories.

Like all families, we had our rituals. For example, as soon as Pa said "amen" at the kitchen table, seven forks were simultaneously thrust at the choicest pieces of chicken that Ma had placed on a large platter before us. Like an old Western movie, the one with the quickest draw came away with the best pieces. Of course, you always ran the risk of being stabbed with a fork, but the risk was worth it in our opinion. We always warned folks, when you ate at the Robertson table, you did so at your own risk.

There was another family ritual that occurred every Sunday morning from the time I was born until the time I left home to enroll at Louisiana Tech. And this particular family habit kind of gives definition to my life even today.

About an hour before Sunday morning worship time, Ma would herd her unruly litter toward whatever rickety car Pa had parked in the ramshackle yard, and all nine of us would squeeze into the first space we could find and head to the little Church of Christ down the road.

In my later teen years, Pa finally broke down and purchased a basic Ford Falcon sedan, the smallest of all Ford models at the time. But we thought we had finally arrived. We were finally rich! Imagine that! The Robertsons proudly tooling around town in a brand-new car!

Looking back, I don't think our neighbors in Dixie, Louisiana, were all that impressed, but we didn't know that then. What did the Robertson family know about wealth? As I said, the car was a basic model with faux leather seats and no air-conditioning. If you are unfamiliar with the relentless humidity and oppressive heat of Louisiana's summers, you cannot appreciate just how scorching hot the inside of a car can get on a sizzling July day. I had one of the boys around here look it up, and when it's 100 degrees outside, the temperature inside a car can get as hot as 172 degrees.

I cannot overstate the scalding that the backside of a young boy's bare legs could take when he came into contact with those vinyl seats. Let's just say, it wasn't pleasant.

But that was our routine, Sunday after Sunday, year in and year out. Get up early, eat a little breakfast, and run a little water through our unkempt hair to smooth it down. The morning drive concluded with the entire clan exploding from that little rig like a pack of rats. I'm not sure of this, but I suspect the respectable church folks quietly muttered to one another, "Well, here comes the Robertson bunch. Something is gonna get torn up today!"

I look back on those days with a certain fondness. In spite of the financial and emotional difficulties our family faced, we were family. Those relationships were an anchor for me that tethered me to the reality that some things are more important than money or the things that money can buy. I had a mother and father who loved me and six siblings who were the center of my universe. Our folks cared enough about our spiritual welfare to take us to church. No matter what happened in life, I knew eight people who would always have my back.

I am also thankful that my folks and the good church people poured the Word of God into my heart. Even though my departure from what they taught me is well documented, it formed the foundation for my later conversion to the Christ-centered life that I am living all these years later.

Tragically, however, even after all of that Bible teaching, I missed something vitally important. Somehow, I escaped my childhood without knowing Jesus. As I've already pointed out, I learned a long list of regulations. Don't dance! Don't drink! Don't cuss! But after all those years of church attendance, I somehow never heard the greatest story ever told.

Oh, I heard the story of the crucifixion, but I had no clear idea about *why* Jesus died. All I heard was some kind of fuzzy narrative about him dying for my sins, but no one ever explained to me what that meant. I definitely heard plenty of hellfire-and-damnation preaching. In fact, it was so ingrained in my psyche that all I knew of God was that he was mad at me. I was certain he didn't like me. And the only thing I knew of the death and resurrection of Jesus was that it was a temporary stay of my death sentence. While all my past sins were forgiven when I was baptized, no one ever told me that God had my future sins covered too.

So, it wasn't too long after my baptism at ten or eleven years old that I sinned again and immediately felt the weight of my death sentence all over again.

Jesus Knows Me—and Loves Me Anyway

Even with all that Bible teaching, I somehow missed the merciful nature of God. I never heard that God loved me! Well, I did hear that he loved me, but the way I heard it, he only loved me when I was good. In fact, I thought he was watching me like a hawk, waiting for me to commit some egregious sin so he could gleefully erase my name from the Book of Life. I never knew that he was driven by his love for me to do the unthinkable on my behalf. I had no idea that he sacrificed his own Son in order to permanently commute my death sentence. I didn't know that his Holy Spirit would live in my body and empower me to walk faithfully with Jesus. And I certainly had no idea that he yearned for me to come to him and live with him. I was completely unaware that he delighted in me.

Yes, I had heard about a man named Jesus, but he wasn't the one I later read about in the Bible, once I started reading it without running everything through the filter of human preachers and teachers. I was shocked to discover the real Jesus is far different from the one they had told me about.

In 1995, Philip Yancey wrote a book provocatively titled *The Jesus I Never Knew.* What an odd title for a book written by a man raised in the kind of evangelical church you see all over the South. In Yancey's day, and in mine, almost everyone identified as a church member. If you've never spent any time down here, you wouldn't know that a man can't turn a corner without bumping into some kind of evangelical church. They're everywhere.

Down here, Christians like to talk about knowing Jesus. That's a noble pursuit, but is it even possible to fully know him? How can a flawed human being with a limited capacity for understanding ever completely grasp a holy and righteous God? And how could a man who does not naturally love others fully and completely comprehend a God who does? How can I wrap my mind around a God who knows every sinful and rebellious thought in my heart and every secret dirty sin and still lays down his life for me?

Nope! Fully and completely knowing God is above my pay grade. If I spent a million years relentlessly poring over volumes of theology books, I would still be no closer to understanding or knowing him than I was when I started.

Fortunately, I don't have to fully know him. What is important is that he fully knows me and that he still fully loves me. That is the point of faith in Jesus. If I could completely understand everything about God that there is to know, he wouldn't be much of a God, would he? So, I just sit back and meditate on the little fragments or glimpses I get of him and marvel at his majesty. What I do know is enough to force me to stand in awe of him, and I hear his voice from Scripture telling me, "My grace is sufficient for you" (2 Cor. 12:9).

This is why I am so passionate about Jesus! A God too big for me to understand has poured out his love into my heart, so I just bask in his glory and grace. I may not be all that smart, and I'm certainly not all that good, but he is both perfectly good and infinitely smart, and that's enough for me.

A God like this is a beautiful God. In fact, he is so beautiful that his beauty outshines everything else that attracts me! My yearning for him is greater than all other cravings. He's just that desirable. I desire him, so I follow him. Where he leads, I try to go. He has everything I want, so if I want something that he doesn't possess, I don't need it or want it.

Jesus the Judge?

The closer I get to the Jesus in the Bible, the more I realize that the one they told me about was otherworldly and unapproachable, with an air about him that sent a very clear message to my heart—*I am too good for you!*

Truthfully, I wanted nothing to do with him.

So when the congregation sang "What a Friend We Have in Jesus," I just couldn't imagine that he and I would ever be friends. I can't really put my finger on what bothered me about him. All I know is that he seemed unreal to me, so surreal in fact that all I wanted to do was to avoid him like the plague. So, I did!

I had no idea there was another Jesus, one who intentionally made a thirty-three-year visit to Planet Earth so I would know that God understands me and that he desires me. I didn't know that he was made just like me, only sinless. I didn't know that he wants me to be comfortable in his presence, to see him as my friend.

This is the problem with a large chunk of the modern church's version of Jesus. He has been reimagined in a way that makes him unavailable to the average person. What Christians have done with Jesus is like the Halloween version of the old reality show *Extreme Makeover.*

He has been made too high and mighty for the average sinner. The prostitutes and the addicts among us scatter when the revised Jesus walks into their community. So does the self-sufficient businessman who's tired of the grind but can't see the relevance of Jesus. Same for the pastor who secretly drinks too much and hates himself for it. Why would anyone want to be friends with someone who seems so far above the worst of us that we could never imagine him hanging out with us?

The answer is we wouldn't. An unapproachable God might possess unimaginable power and authority, but if I can't allow him to see the flawed nature of my humanity, what kind of God is he? The only thing a God like that can do for me is pile another unhealthy, soul-killing, life-destroying dose of judgment on me.

Thanks, but no thanks!

I've heard of people who, in the deepest depths of despair about their sin and brokenness, still reject invitations to church because they're convinced the people there would just make them feel even worse about themselves and their situation. Now, some of these people might want to avoid church for the same reason that Adam and Eve ran from God after they disobeyed him. Their guilt was a stark reminder that they were morally filthy. I don't know, maybe that's why sinners at the very end of their rope still avoid God's people. But I suspect their reluctance to go to God's people for help has as much to do with the Jesus that these church people have invented as it does with any sinner's sense of his own guilt and shame.

However, I find it almost impossible to read the four gospel accounts of Jesus' life and not clearly see that his mercy is greater than any sin. If anyone really sees the Jesus I know, they wouldn't run from him. Instead, they would hurdle every obstacle to get to him. Nothing would keep them from reaching that Jesus.

If anyone really sees the Jesus I know, they wouldn't run from him.

Why Reinvent Him?

If the authentic Jesus is so good, why reinvent him? That is a very good question.

The answer, in part, is a spiritual truth that is so contrary to our spirit of independence that we will do whatever we can do to avoid it. I'm talking about the fact that every single one of us is in the same sinking boat as those people we consider to be the worst of sinners. We are all lawbreakers. Every one of us is, down to the last man and woman.

> For whoever keeps the whole law and yet stumbles at just one point
> is guilty of breaking all of it. (James 2:10)

I've been reading that passage for a long time, and I don't see any legal loopholes in it. Do you? I know I don't get a pass on this just because I've never snorted cocaine or smoked crystal meth. But I'm still a lawbreaker because I've broken the law of God in other areas. The news is really bad for me, since I didn't break just one law. I broke almost all of his commandments at one time or another.

So, unless you are absolutely and flawlessly perfect, you are also a criminal standing in the court of the Most High God, and you have no defense. That includes you, me, and the prostitute. God isn't going to pat you on the back and say, *I know you coveted your neighbor's wife a time or two, but at least you didn't rob banks. I'll let you off this time since you aren't as bad as that person.*

No, we are all guilty! And we would have stayed guilty if God had not done something unthinkable to intervene and take away our guilt. We, however, would rather do it on our own. We would prefer to point to our own goodness as proof that we have earned a spot on the team. So, we mold a new Jesus who didn't come to save sinners but to give us a little moral boost.

The problem with that Jesus is that he is impotent, completely powerless to extinguish the fires of hell that burn in our hearts when we are separated from the Almighty because of our sin. He can't do us any good at all.

The God of Mercy

We don't need a little help; instead, we are in desperate need of the absolute unlimited mercy of God. We need a do-over!

> You were taught, with regard to your former way of life, to put off your old self, which is being corrupted by its deceitful desires; to be made new in the attitude of your minds; and to put on the new self, created to be like God in true righteousness and holiness. (Eph. 4:22–24)

Thankfully, the Almighty is a good God who delights in lavishly dispensing his grace. And he doesn't pour it out on good people, since good people don't need mercy. Instead, he lavishes it on lawbreakers who have already had their death sentence pronounced. It is for people who see it as their last and only hope. People like me!

Once we know that, it does two things for those who desire his grace. It changes who we are, and it changes how we view other sinners. While we realize that God is repulsed by sin, it also allows us to know that there is no wrongdoing so disgusting that it would make God say, *Okay, you've crossed the line now! My mercy only goes so far! You're done!*

We may operate like that, but not Jesus. He is the one, after all, who said,

"Come to me, all you who are weary and burdened, and I will give you rest. Take my yoke upon you and learn from me, for I am gentle and humble in heart, and you will find rest for your souls." (Matt. 11:28–29)

I would like to tell you about the worst day of my life, but the only problem is, there isn't a single worst day. It was more like a long string of worst days. In fact, for most of my life, until I met Jesus, I was one miserable son of a gun.

But there was a day where the futile life I once lived came face-to-face with the life God had created me to live.

In between the time my sister Jan had dragged the pastor to my bar and the day of my awakening, the ugly truth about me had really taken root in a new way. The fruit of sin's seed that was planted in my heart began to bear even more fruit. I got worse before I got better. Way worse!

Every time I looked at Miss Kay and the boys, it was an ugly reminder of how far I had fallen. When I saw my faithful and loving wife and my boys, it only served to remind me of what a miserable failure I was in every area of my life that mattered. So, I did what I thought would give me some relief. In a fit of rage, I ordered Miss Kay to leave me: "Get your stuff and those kids and get out of here."

In 2023, my nephew Zach and my son Willie released a movie about my conversion to Christ. Our family and a couple hundred other friends were sitting in the theater for the family premiere, and someone asked me, "Phil, are you excited to see the finished product?"

Sarcastically, I replied, "Oh, yeah! I get to see every rotten, filthy deed I ever did displayed on the big screen."

Truthfully, the scene where I ran Kay and the boys out of the house was the hardest to watch. It was a vivid reminder of how "corruptible" I am without the Spirit of God living in me.

I understand now that it was an illogical move on my part, because rather than finding freedom from responsibility, I was in greater bondage to my sin. God moved even further away from me. I didn't hear God's literal voice, but after consistently reading and studying the Bible over the last fifty years, I realize now that God was saying, *Okay, Phil, you want independence? You now have it. Let's see how that works out for you.*

Yet, at the very moment I was at my weakest, I heard him say, *Come to me and I will give you rest.* In spite of my weary sloshing through the mire of my sin, and in spite of the increasingly heavy burden I was carrying, he called me to come to him.

Do you want to know what Jesus did not say to me? He didn't say, "Come to my church! Come to my organization! Come to my ministry!" Instead, he invited me to himself. I needed the brothers and sisters in the church, but "Come to me" is a vastly different plea than

"Get yourself back in church!" One calls me to a place and the other to a person. Big difference!

Once we finally discover that this holy and infinite God invites us to come to him personally, there are only two ways to respond. Either we refuse his invitation, or we accept it.

The Powerful Testimony of a Changed Life

Paul was a fellow who spent his earlier years tormenting believers, throwing them into prison and having them stoned to death. But meeting Jesus changed him.

> So from now on we regard no one from a worldly point of view. Though we once regarded Christ in this way, we do so no longer. Therefore, if anyone is in Christ, the new creation has come: The old has gone, the new is here! All this is from God, who reconciled us to himself through Christ. (2 Cor. 5:16–18)

It's ironic, isn't it? Until God blinded Paul, he was unable to see the infinite value of either Christ or those who followed him. Until that moment, he viewed people from a worldly point of view. Either they fit into the agenda of the Pharisees or they didn't. If they didn't, he went after them (Acts 9:1–22).

However, once Paul had an encounter with the risen Jesus on the road to Damascus, he became a new man. A new creation. God reconciled Paul to himself, the same God he had rebelled against. How ironic that he was saved by the blood of the very Christ he had been trying to destroy. The only thing Paul did to contribute to his new life in Jesus was to fall on his face in sheer terror.

Paul's view of Jesus changed when he met Jesus, but so did his view of sinners. No longer interested in destroying them, he worked to break the demonic chains that kept them in spiritual prison. I heard someone say, "Hurt people hurt people." I agree with that assessment. But I would also say that redeemed people redeem people. This is what the Bible says about that:

> Be merciful to those who doubt; save others by snatching them from the fire; to others show mercy, mixed with fear—hating even the clothing stained by corrupted flesh. (Jude vv. 22–23)

This is how I try to live, because I don't want it on my conscience that someone's life was destroyed by Satan and I never even opened my mouth about Jesus. What kind of Jesus follower would I be if I saw someone struggling with the weariness of sin and I didn't tell them about the man who said, "Come to me . . . and I will give you rest" (Matt. 11:28)?

Paul himself was not satisfied to just have his own sins washed away. Being saved meant he took on the mission that God gives all Christians.

> God . . . gave us the ministry of reconciliation: that God was reconciling the world to himself in Christ, not counting people's sins against them. And he has committed to us the message of reconciliation. We

are therefore Christ's ambassadors, as though God were making his appeal through us. We implore you on Christ's behalf: Be reconciled to God. God made him who had no sin to be sin for us, so that in him we might become the righteousness of God. (2 Cor. 5:18–21)

A church in the Midwest recently put this encouraging message on their church sign: "Whoever stole our AC unit, keep it. It's hot where you are going."

What a great message for the people of God to proclaim to the lost (please note the sarcasm). The gist of our good brethren's message was, "We will gleefully stand by as eternal flames lick your flesh." If that doesn't help the thieves to see the love of God, I don't know what will (again, note the sarcasm).

Perhaps the good people at that church should reevaluate their priorities. Like, I don't know, maybe becoming what we were born again to be, namely, ambassadors of reconciliation. Paul said that God makes his appeal through us, so perhaps this church should get busy with that little task.

There is no ambiguity in Paul's message in 2 Corinthians. If you are confused about this, look at his language again: "the ministry of reconciliation," "not counting people's sins against them," "Christ's ambassadors," "God . . . making his appeal through us," "we implore you," "be reconciled to God."

Not more than a day or two goes by that I don't get a call from someone who is at the end of their rope. They walk into my house or meet me at the building where some of God's family assembles and hope they can find some relief. Often, they have tried the "Jesus thing." The only problem is, they haven't met the Jesus in the Scriptures.

More often than not, they are shocked when I tell them about the Jesus of the Bible. Like I was at one time, they have no idea that the real Jesus is on their side. They never heard the good news that he actually desires to wash their guilt away and draw them into a lifelong friendship with him.

I'm just thinking perhaps that church sign should have read, "To whoever stole our AC unit: Show up here on Sunday morning and let us introduce you to the real Jesus. He can set you free!"

The message of the Bible is that Jesus drank the cup of wrath that had our name on it, and we get to drink the cup of mercy. So, if we really believe this is true, what is the loss of an air conditioner really worth when compared to introducing sinners to the only one who can rescue them from hell? I would much prefer to let the thieves know that Christ died for them so that their sins wouldn't be counted against them.

In a broken, sin-cursed world where Satan lives as an opportunistic predator, he is an expert at using guilt and shame to take us captive to do his will. He does this by preying on our shame, reminding us that we have crossed the line with God, that we are too far gone for a holy God. He does what he can to deceive "those who are perishing" (1 Cor. 1:18) into believing that God is not a good god.

When Jesus came on the scene, and the devil orchestrated his murder, Satan thought he had God by the throat. However, I suspect he gasped in horror when the body of Jesus was reenergized with new life and he was raised from the grave. It had to be the greatest "Uh-oh, I've done it now" moment in all of cosmic history.

This is the story I tell: the real Jesus willingly submitted himself to Satan's master plan to kill him. I just point others to the real Jesus who died for scumbags like them and like me. I tell them about the God of all hope (Rom. 15:13) and the God of all comfort (2 Cor. 1:3–5). I do my best to clear out the underbrush that prevents them from seeing the brilliance of the light of God and his resurrection from the dead.

So far, all of this may sound theoretical. But if you want to put skin on it, I would encourage you again to read the Gospels of Matthew, Mark, Luke, and John. There, you will see a Jesus you may have never heard about. You will see a Messiah who is kind and compassionate in how he deals with the downtrodden. He simply pleaded with the crowds, "Be with me! Follow me! Begin the process of becoming like me! Do your best to do what I do!"

It's Time to Lawyer Up

One account of how Jesus treated sinners is found in the eighth chapter of John's gospel. Jesus was holding an early morning Bible study when a group of Jewish religious leaders dragged a woman before him who had been caught in the act of adultery.

Let's focus on this scene for a moment. "Caught in the act" means that someone burst through this woman's door and caught her naked in bed with a man other than her husband. The apostle John doesn't tell us, but I don't think it's a stretch to imagine they dragged her through the streets butt naked. And by the time they threw her down like a dog at Jesus' feet, she was probably covered with grime sticking to her hot, sweaty flesh.

I covered this in more detail in my last book, *Uncanceled*, but this passage is pivotal in helping us to see the real Jesus. The theologians were partially correct in saying that the law commanded the woman to be executed, but the law also said that the man she was consorting with should die too. That was the law.

But these pastors didn't give a rip about either the woman or the law's instructions on what to do with adulterers. Not really! They only wanted to catch Jesus in a theological trap.

Why? It was because he bypassed their institutions and made God available to the masses without having to go through their religious system.

They tried to make a legal argument, but Jesus didn't take the bait. He didn't utter a word about the law in response. I mean, he could have since he was the author of the law of Moses. Instead, he chose to point the woman and her accusers to a higher law, that is, the *law of mercy*.

Jesus didn't defend her adultery or any other sin. We know this is true because the last thing he told the woman was, "Go now and leave your life of sin" (John 8:11). But before he gave her the charge to live a godly life, he had to first absolve her of her shame. How could a woman just "caught in the act of adultery" worship God, for crying out loud? She was far too filthy for that! Before she could approach God and hold her hands up in praise, someone would have to make her clean again.

Jesus straightened up and asked her, "Woman, where are they? Has no one condemned you?"

"No one, sir," she said.

"Then neither do I condemn you." (vv. 10–11)

In the case of this woman, he didn't suspend the law, but he defended her on the basis of mercy. Instead of directly responding to the accusations of the teachers of the law and the Pharisees, he simply stooped to the ground and began to scribble in the dirt.

John didn't give us a clue about how long he wrote in the dirt or what he wrote. Perhaps he was writing the names of the women with whom some of the Pharisees had themselves committed adultery. But whatever he wrote, it apparently turned his next statement into a nuclear bomb that blew their self-righteousness to kingdom come.

"The sinless one among you, go first. Throw the stone" (John 8:7 THE MESSAGE).

Ouch! "You sinless ones go first?" That had to hurt! Talk about taking a fire hose to douse the flames of condemnation. Even the most godly people in the world, even after years of practicing religion, can't get away from one cold, hard fact: *we all still sin.* Maybe not as much as we once did, but we still sin, nonetheless.

We know the Pharisees and teachers of the law got the point because, one by one, they dropped their rocks and walked away with their heads bowed low.

I've never been charged with a crime (even though I should have been), but if I ever stand before a judge and jury, I want this lawyer defending me.

Speaking of lawyers, you may actually be surprised to discover that one of the roles Jesus fills is to act as our celestial defense attorney. One of his jobs (for lack of a better term) is to defend us against the accusations that are brought against us by Satan.

My dear children, I write this to you so that you will not sin. But if anybody does sin, we have an advocate with the Father—Jesus Christ, the Righteous One. (1 John 2:1)

We can't have Jesus without having a growing hatred for sin. Following Jesus means that I learn to hate sin as much as he does. But the Almighty knows us, fully understands us, and he is completely aware of our tendency to do the wrong thing. Paraphrasing the above verse from 1 John, the Holy Spirit is telling us, "Don't sin! But if you do sin, you still have a defense attorney, Jesus Christ. He will plead your case before the judge, and he wins 100 percent of his cases!"

Does God require us to lawyer up before he'll let us in? Or is it we who need to know that we have someone representing us in heaven before we can approach him?

I'll leave the answer to the theologians, but I do know Jesus told this woman, "Neither do I condemn you" (John 8:11). I also know this, that in her case, she didn't need to explain herself before God. I mean, he was standing

We can't have Jesus without having a growing hatred for sin.

there, right in front of her. Not only did Jesus know she was a sinner, but he also knew she was fully aware of her guilt. She already felt condemned enough, so what good would it have done for Jesus to continue to point that fact out? What she needed was a defender, a lawyer.

I'm glad this passage is in the Bible because I've heard those voices of condemnation myself. More than once. Whenever anyone accuses me of sin, it sticks to me like glue. Whatever Satan accuses me of, I'm defenseless. And when I make my plea, it is always *guilty*!

So, if I am going to survive Satan's relentless assault against my inner desire to be liberated from his control, it is absolutely necessary that I know that my defender is capable of doing his job.

Thankfully, I have Jesus' word on this: "If the Son sets you free, you will be free indeed" (John 8:36).

The Only Pathway to Real Liberty

On October 28, 1886, the people of France presented the United States with the Statue of Liberty. The statue depicts Libertas, the Roman goddess of liberty. At the base of the statue is a tablet inscribed with these now famous words:

> Give me your tired, your poor,
> Your huddled masses yearning to breathe free,
> The wretched refuse of your teeming shore.

Don't get me wrong, I love America. I've traveled around the globe a bit, and when I return to the United States, I notice I breathe a little freer. I do value that.

However, we have fallen short of perfect liberty for everyone. I'll discuss this elsewhere, but there is no shortage of examples of how America has failed to live up to its promise of offering freedom to every tired, poor, wretched soul who yearns to be free.

As appealing as Libertas's promise of freedom may seem to us, she is powerless to deliver on it. The inscription on her statue sounds good to us, but she can't really offer real freedom. She isn't even a real god, for crying out loud.

Thankfully, there is another God who actually can take the tired, poor, and huddled masses and liberate them from their bondage to mortality. He can set them free from the chains of sin and allow them to live in intimate fellowship with the God who created them. His name is Jesus.

And most of all, he can eliminate the shame and guilt that prevent us all from approaching a holy, all-powerful, majestic God like the God of the Bible. When shame hobbles us before the throne, we can take comfort in knowing that Jesus is answering the accusations of the great accuser. He is speaking out in our defense. Being defended by our attorney, who has never lost a case, empowers us to go directly to the Father with absolute confidence that he will welcome us.

Tired, poor, huddled masses? Oh, yeah! Our yearning for freedom has finally come to fruition in Jesus.

six

JESUS, THE SERVANT

*After that, he poured water into a basin
and began to wash his disciples' feet.*

JOHN 13:5

I found an interesting tidbit of useless information recently. King Charles III of Great Britain has almost five hundred personal assistants and servants.[1] I'm not sure what Charles does with his time, but he must be an important man to have that many people at his beck and call.

I have never given it much thought, but in some ways, having people to do the stuff that normal people do for themselves is supposedly an indicator of status. It signals to the rest of us that they are several rungs above us on society's ladder.

But let's not be too hard on Charlie. We all love our status symbols, don't we? Around these parts, the more disabled trucks, cars, and four-wheelers you have in your overgrown yard, the more people tend to think you've finally made it. I'm not saying my yard is the worst in the area, but I can assure you I'll never win the yard-of-the-month award.

If you want to project status down here in the bowels of Ouachita Parish's Ninth Ward, an unkempt yard is where you start. But if you truly want to be the envy of your neighbors, you will also need a personal assistant, a manservant. You know, someone to clean your fish and game, to kill your wasps and snakes, to make a run to Walmart for you. Once you get to this level, you're at the top of the redneck food chain.

The Status of a Wealthy Servant King

Status is important to most people, but not so much with God. This got me to wondering, *What if there was another way to think about status, a way that more accurately reflects the Almighty's nature?*

As it turns out, there is a king who is nothing like any leader you've ever heard of. A wealthy monarch who owns all of the wealth of the entire universe. He possesses infinite authority and power and forms galaxies and universes with a command.

> "I have no need of a bull from your stall
> or of goats from your pens,
> for every animal of the forest is mine,
> and the cattle on a thousand hills.

I know every bird in the mountains,

and the insects in the fields are mine.

If I were hungry I would not tell you,

for the world is mine, and all that is in it." (Ps. 50:9–12)

Is it a stretch to call a king like this the King of kings, the Lord of lords? In my estimation, these are good titles for a being so mighty and so glorious that all of his qualities are limitless. With infinite power, glory, wealth, and goodness, he is far above all other rulers.

I think that *King of kings* fits a king like this one. What about you?

Imagine that Jesus had waited until the 2020s to make his appearance. Furthermore, imagine that you had just signed up to be one of his closest advisors. And then you get the email: "The King of kings has elected to forgo all status symbols. He has abandoned his castle and his throne. He no longer has personal assistants and servants. Instead, he has turned our expectations upside down and has chosen to live his life rendering service to his servants."

What a scandal! What a preposterous idea! The king serving his subjects? Who would believe a story like that?

Now you know why so many of us have a tough time finding God. His upside-down approach to status destroys our attitudes about success, rank, and position. If you treasure the things that can be destroyed, this has to be the worst news ever. The king is here, ready to claim his throne, but instead he's walking around and acting like the lowliest of servants.

To be honest, this goes against everything I once thought I wanted in a king. When I thought of what a good king would look like, he actually looked a lot like what I wanted myself to be. And that was my problem! I didn't want a king as much as I wanted to *be* king.

And now you know why I rejected Jesus as king for so long. I wanted the job for myself. I wanted the authority. I wanted to run my own life. And even if I did ever consider putting myself under someone else's kingship, at least let it be one who offers to give me what I want.

But a king, a God, a supreme, all-powerful deity who allows his subjects to brutalize and murder him? A story like that certainly didn't fit my vision of what a king ought to be. Nor did it match the vision I had for my adult life when I was a kid. Not even a little bit!

I've given you the short version, a synopsis of Jesus' mission. But you don't have to take my word for it. The Gospels of Matthew, Mark, Luke, and John can flesh out this story in greater detail. But make no mistake. It is an incredibly powerful story that, if true, will change the direction of a person's life.

There's an interesting scene in Matthew's gospel where Jesus' disciples were arguing about who would be first in his coming kingdom. Of course, they were thinking of palaces, armies, and a well-organized government. I'm not being critical of his boys since there is no way they could have known at this point just what Jesus was up to. I'm not sure I would have either. Maybe I'm taking too much liberty with the Scriptures, but I can imagine it now: James and John's mom calling Jesus off to the side and whispering, "Jesus, do you think it's possible for John to be your secretary of state and James to be your secretary of defense?"

Their mother was not unlike most mothers. She only wanted the best for her sons. Important positions for her sons elevated her status too. We may chuckle at how presumptuous she was, but we get it. This desire to see our kids succeed is what drives fanatic parents to pace up and down the sidelines of youth football games and yell at their children to step up their performance on the field. Even though common sense would tell you that only a tiny fraction of all the children in America who participate in youth sports will go to college on an athletic scholarship, we still push our kids harder to perform.

Yes, the mother of these two disciples was like plenty of parents in the world. She dreamed of boasting to her friends, when they all gathered at the public watering hole, "You know, my boys are the king's most important advisors."

I kind of chuckle at the other disciples who were so indignant at James and John. They weren't offended that this woman asked for her sons to get the best seats in Jesus' kingdom. Instead, they were upset that James and John's mother had beaten them to the punch!

Positions of power and influence. It is tempting to chase after those things, isn't it?

But while it is true that Jesus came to be crowned king, it wasn't what these misfits were looking for. They wanted what the Pharisees had: the praise of the common folk. They wanted the best seats at the parties and to be greeted with respect in public.

Much to their chagrin, Jesus' coronation was far different from that of King David, or even King Charles III. He was an upside-down kind of king, one who would rule in a way that would be at odds with how mankind thinks kings should rule. Only the Twelve didn't know it yet.

His response to them must have stung a little.

"You know that the rulers of the Gentiles lord it over them, and their high officials exercise authority over them. Not so with you. Instead, whoever wants to become great among you must be your servant, and whoever wants to be first must be your slave—just as the Son of Man did not come to be served, but to serve, and to give his life as a ransom for many." (Matt. 20:25–28)

"What? So you're saying that no special places of honor or expensive robes are waiting for us? Are you telling us that we don't get to be in charge of people?"

They didn't get it then, but what Jesus told them in this passage would lead eleven of them to eventually die a martyr's death. In essence, he was telling them that yes, he did come to rule, but his rule would be a spiritual one founded on a man who had a servant spirit. As I said, this was a shock, not only that he was a serving God, but that he was calling them to the same ministry. Talk about upsetting their applecart! This had to be a gut punch to this group of boys who had a more radical and violent expectation of what God's kingdom would be like.

Their king was demanding them to embrace the life of servanthood! An upside-down life!

The one on the top is really on the bottom, and the one on the bottom is really on the top!

What nonsense this must have sounded like to them at first. It went against all of their hopes and expectations.

But as the biography of Jesus unfolds in the Gospels, we find that he came to destroy only one enemy, and it wasn't the Romans or the Jewish leaders. He was on a mission to destroy death.

An Approachable King

I have no idea what King Charles is like when he is alone with his family. But in public, he seems aloof and detached, even unapproachable. I wonder the same thing about the presidents and prime ministers we see in the news. What are they like in private? I know one thing: we don't often get the sense they are here to serve their constituents. Whether it's true or not, it's sometimes easy to get the idea they are in it for what they can get.

Not so with Jesus. Like presidents and kings, he was surrounded by a group of hangers-on. Unlike them, however, he didn't use his followers for his own political benefit. They weren't his pawns but his friends. He didn't leverage them for his own good. Instead, he loved them as he loved himself (Matt. 22:37–40).

Now that's different! You certainly don't see that every day! Kings befriending low-income common folks.

To give us an idea of just how lowly and humble the Creator of the cosmos made himself, we need to look at a scene that unfolds in the thirteenth chapter of John's gospel. It shatters all of our illusions about gods and kings. Only a few days before his death, King Jesus did the unthinkable.

The evening meal was in progress, and the devil had already prompted Judas, the son of Simon Iscariot, to betray Jesus. Jesus knew that the Father had put all things under his power, and that he had come from God and was returning to God; so he got up from the meal, took off his outer clothing, and wrapped a towel around

his waist. After that, he poured water into a basin and began to wash
his disciples' feet, drying them with the towel that was wrapped
around him. (vv. 2–5)

Who is this guy on his knees? A hired hand? A slave? Surely he isn't
a king! Kings have *their* feet washed. They don't perform menial tasks
like foot washing. It would be unthinkable to find a king stooping so
low. Who is he?

The answer to that question is at the heart of the gospel. Who is
this man, Jesus? He is the God who spoke atoms and molecules into
existence. He is the God who breathed out stars and galaxies and this
incredibly vast universe. He is the God who created you and me in his
own image. He is the God who restored sight to the blind and raised
the dead. A miracle worker.

As incredible as it may seem, that's the man who was down on
his knees, a towel wrapped around his waist, washing the feet of his
followers. Almighty God, serving the very same people he created.
Don't let this pass you by, because this passage puts skin on the nature
of God. We can speak of him in lofty theological language, but it can
all be reduced to this scene. God in the flesh washing feet!

To the Jewish theologians and to all other religions, this is a scan-
dalous scene. No one in his right mind would have God the Creator
doing such lowly work, especially serving people like this sniveling,
complaining, impulsive group of boys who were perhaps barely out
of puberty.

But if the Bible is an accurate biography of Jesus, the significance
of what we are reading is undeniable. We can't escape the fact that the

God who is all-knowing, all-powerful, and is everywhere at once is getting his hands dirty doing the work of a servant.

In the second chapter of Philippians, the apostle Paul expounds on the idea that God is a servant to mankind.

In your relationships with one another, have the same mindset as Christ Jesus:

> Who, being in very nature God,
>   did not consider equality with God something to be
>   used to his own advantage;
> rather, he made himself nothing
>   by taking the very nature of a servant,
>   being made in human likeness.
> And being found in appearance as a man,
>   he humbled himself
>   by becoming obedient to death—
>   even death on a cross! (vv. 5–8)

You've got to be kidding me! What an incredible, unbelievable story. God taking on the flesh of humanity. The same humanity he created? And then to top it off, he appeared on the world's stage as a newborn baby? In a barn, no less? Then he grew up the son of a carpenter and went on to serve humanity by submitting to bearing their sins on a Roman cross? Taking on the nature of a servant?

Nah! It's not possible!

I said it's unbelievable, and to many it is. But the sheer fact that it goes against the grain of everything we would do if we were to make up our own god makes me believe it more. It is so counterintuitive that only someone far superior to you and me could come up with this wild tale.

This, however, begs another question. Why would he do such a thing? Why not just give us what we deserve and roast us in the flames?

That is a very good question, and the answer to it tells us everything else we need to know about God. Paul gives us a good answer in the second chapter of Ephesians:

> Because of his great love for us, God, who is rich in mercy, made us alive with Christ even when we were dead in transgressions. (vv. 4–5)

Before he came on the scene, our prospects were pretty dismal. Dead in our sins . . . "without hope and without God in the world" (v. 12). Jesus did what he did so we could become "'children of God without fault in a warped and crooked generation'" (Phil. 2:15).

In other words, he did what was impossible for us to do for ourselves: to remove the guilt that leads to our death. And Jesus did it for one reason: "Because of his great love for us" (Eph. 2:4). If he did not love us, he would have just pronounced the sentence we deserve—death in flames—and gone on about the business of being God. Instead, he served out our sentence for us.

Not only was my arrest warrant ripped up, but there isn't even a record of my crimes in any database anywhere on earth or in heaven. When I believed in him, Jesus' blood was used as a sort of cosmic cleansing agent and my rap sheet was erased. You can't find it anymore. It's as if it never existed. We might recall some of the details of our rebellious past, but God has no recollection of any of it.

> "This is the covenant I will make with them
>> after that time, says the Lord.
> I will put my laws in their hearts,
>> and I will write them on their minds."

Then he adds:

> "Their sins and lawless acts
>> I will remember no more." (Heb. 10:16–17)

Whether or not a sovereign God can actually forget something is a discussion I will leave to the theologians. But one thing is clear: because of the fact that a servant God humbled himself and paid off my sin account, God will never hold my sin against me. Past, present, or future sins—they're all gone! Eradicated! Erased! Nailed to the cross!

Some hear this incredible story of hope and think, *Good! I'm glad all of my sins are taken care of! Now I don't have to be so careful about how I live my life since I have an unlimited expense account.*

That would be a mistake. Paul dealt with this idea in a number of places. One is in his letter to the Romans.

God will never hold my sin against me.

121

Someone might argue, "If my falsehood enhances God's truthfulness and so increases his glory, why am I still condemned as a sinner?" Why not say—as some slanderously claim that we say—"Let us do evil that good may result"? Their condemnation is just! (3:7–8)

The actual value of Jesus' sacrifice for our sins is immeasurable. It is offered free of charge, since we can't pay for it anyhow. But the deal does have a catch, if you can call it that. It is only open to one kind of person: the people who have come to understand that everything they've invested in up to the point they hear the gospel is worthless. It's only when we begin to grasp the futility of life without the God who created us that we are ready to enter into a relationship with him.

I say that it has a catch, but it isn't really much of a catch if you consider that God is offering to resurrect us from death and gift us with eternal life. This requires us to do one thing in response: to follow Jesus! It's not a deal-breaker for me, though, because I'm trading in what's worthless for what is infinitely valuable. To tell the truth, I didn't do such a good job of living a good life before I met him.

So, when Jesus said that he didn't come to be served but to serve and offer his life as a ransom for many, he is calling anyone who yearns to be ransomed from the Evil One's control to follow him. In other words, ransomed people are motivated to imitate the one who ransomed them. We want to be like him as much as we can.

When we begin our apprenticeship under him, we are called upon to imitate him in every way, but especially in his desire to serve others. He didn't come to pump our gas, even though he may have done that. He didn't even come primarily to wash our feet.

Remember, his purpose in coming was to serve us by doing the one thing for us that we could never do for ourselves. He came to take the beating that we deserved (Isa. 53:5). Foot washing wasn't the main point here, but it was a symbol of his purpose, that God would humble himself by serving others and provide for us in our spiritual poverty.

I thank him that he rescued me from the kingdom of darkness and death, that's for sure. Left to my own power and ability, I would be dead in my sins and trespasses still (Col. 1:13).

To Be with Him

I don't want to beat a dead horse, but I do want to make sure that we haven't moved on from this topic before we drive this point home: the purpose of Jesus' death wasn't just to give us a "Get Out of Hell Free" card. It was way more than that. He died to save us from both the penalty of sin and the control of sin. He died to destroy the impenetrable barrier between us and God.

While it is true that Christ died to save us from our sins, he essentially saved us from ourselves, from our tendency to do our own thing, to follow our own instincts, from the things that lead to death. This independent spirit is man's default position in the universe, and it infects us with a terminal illness. When we sin, we die (Ezek. 18:20), and we can trace this trail of death from Adam and Eve to the present age. We are all under a cloud of judgment because of it.

Rebellion against God, a spirit of disobedience, trying to be lord and master of our own destiny? That's our nature.

There's really no serious debate that we are wicked creatures prone to do evil. If you doubt that, you don't get out much. You certainly don't watch the news. (If you don't watch the news, I don't blame you! It's a depressing narrative that mankind is writing about itself.) But we can't argue with a straight face that we are good. We just aren't, and we all know it.

The reason that we can't be good on our own is that Satan capitalizes on our desire to be independent of God and uses it to lead us into death. We're pretty good at doing his bidding on this. In fact, every one of us, down to the last human being on Planet Earth, has taken Satan's bait. Look at what Jesus said about Satan: "The thief comes only to steal and kill and destroy" (John 10:10).

No doubt about it! How many break-ins has he committed in your community, in your family? Broken marriages? Addicted family members? Young men and women confused about their gender and sexuality? Lives ruined by gossip and slander?

There are plenty of Christians who are experts at pointing out that we are under the control of the Evil One (1 John 5:19). As a matter of fact, I don't shy away from this truth myself. As I often say, we can't appreciate the good news until we know just how bad the bad news is. But if that's where Christians stopped, people would still be under Satan's control. Finding out that you have cancer is bad news, but when your doctor tells you that he has a treatment plan with a 100 percent success rate? Now that is good news!

We are (or were) all under a sentence of death. But don't let people walk away from your message until they get an opportunity to hear that God has a plan to cure their spiritual cancer. Before you let them go, they need to know about the one who can raise them from the dead.

"I have come that they may have life, and have it to the full." (John 10:10)

This is how he serves us! He does it by restoring order to our chaos. He serves us by raising us from the dead and restoring us to the life we were created to live. Ultimately, he serves us by bringing us back into the life of God (Eph. 4:18).

Therefore, I have a question for you that gets to the bottom line of how Jesus best serves us. If his purpose is to give us the life of God, the abundant life, where would we find this life? The obvious answer is that we find the life of God in the presence of God. This means that just dying for our sins was not the primary goal of his ministry. Instead, it is that he died for our sins so that we can comfortably enter into God's presence.

No more controlling guilt and shame. They're gone, along with our reluctance to approach God freely and confidently.

When we begin to understand this, we can easily see how this is more than a "Get Out of Hell Free" card. Instead, it is a passport into the throne room of God, where true life is to be found.

We find the life of God in the presence of God.

Be with Jesus, Begin to Do What
Jesus Did, Become Like Jesus

Recently, an *Unashamed* podcast listener responded to one of my newsletters, saying that he had serious doubts about where he stood with God, based on the fact that he had not yet had a religious experience. Apparently, some of his well-meaning friends had told him about their experiences, saying they had received an inner feeling of some kind.

I don't doubt that God spoke to his friends' hearts in this way, but this is not God's primary goal. Besides, as I pointed out to this listener, feelings are poor indicators of what is real, since they are so unreliable. So, I shared a few Bible verses with him that would make it plain that his goal should be to seek what God has already revealed, particularly about what God's purpose is for his life. That's something we can bank on, and it has nothing to do with how or what we feel. I told him about God's reliable, trustworthy revelation. God has revealed only one purpose for us, one goal to free us up from the tension that prevents us from being with God. God desires to live in us and help us live freely and unashamedly with him. God isn't telling us to become instantly perfect before we can live with him; instead, he tells us to enter into his apprenticeship program and be mentored by the greatest servant to ever live.

And all of that is a process that will go on until we breathe our last breath. After that, we physically enter into the throne room of God with our resurrected flesh to live eternally with him in perfect union.

So, yes! When we come to God by the power of the blood of Christ, we are changed. What was once important loses its luster when what used to be unimportant to us becomes our passion. Living with God inside of us makes us different than we once were. I'm not just talking about the obvious things like stopping cussing, drinking, running around, gossiping, and backbiting! What I mean is that we begin to be more like Jesus just because we've been hanging around him and listening to what he says and does. We become imitators of Jesus because of the incredible spiritual gifts he has lavished on us.

It is true that following Jesus means that we begin to put away the filthy deeds of the flesh (Col. 3:8; Rom. 1:26–32; Gal. 5:19–21; 1 Cor. 6:9–11). But more than that, it means we also become servants of our fellow man in the same way that Jesus was. This is exactly what Jesus said after he had washed the feet of his disciples:

> When he had finished washing their feet, he put on his clothes and returned to his place. "Do you understand what I have done for you?" he asked them. "You call me 'Teacher' and 'Lord,' and rightly so, for that is what I am. Now that I, your Lord and Teacher, have washed your feet, you also should wash one another's feet. I have set you an example that you should do as I have done for you. Very truly I tell you, no servant is greater than his master, nor is a messenger greater than the one who sent him. Now that you know these things, you will be blessed if you do them." (John 13:12–17)

The argument Jesus made in this story is plain. "If I, the Creator of the cosmos, became a servant to you, then you must commit your life to the same kind of self-sacrifice on behalf of one another. You must take on the role of the servant by becoming what your friends need for you to become: a proclaimer of life-giving truth."

I would argue that we are never more like Jesus than when we are serving others. This is what I told the young man who responded to my newsletter. I encouraged him to:

1. walk with Jesus,
2. then become like Jesus, by the power of the indwelling God!
3. and finally, do what Jesus did when he was here on this planet.

These are the three steps, if you want to call them that, to experiencing the life of God. Just spend your life following Jesus, and you'll soon be more like him than you ever thought possible.

How we treat others, how willing we are to lay down our lives for our fellow man is the most important indicator that we are being transformed to become more like Jesus. We serve people, even when they are steeped in disgusting sin. We speak the truth of God to them, even when they won't listen. We serve them, even when they would rather do it themselves. And we love them even when they hate us!

When you agree to be transformed into the image of God's Son (Rom. 8:29), you will find you are finally at peace with God. No more hostility! No more fear that God won't take you in! You'll know that you are okay with God, because you will be walking with Jesus, the Son of God.

Talk about having an experience! This is it. It may or may not be a flash of light that knocks you off your feet and blinds you for three days, like Paul experienced on the road to Damascus. Instead, it may begin like Peter's experience, when he heard the rooster crow and immediately knew he had betrayed his Lord. That was the beginning of his pathway to servant leadership. He was never the same after that.

One thing I know, however, is that an experience like this only increases in intensity the more you walk with Jesus and become more like Jesus. The only decision any of us must make is to choose between two roads. Either we will walk the broad road of self-realization and self-service, or we will travel the narrow road of servanthood.

We should all be careful how we choose, however, because one way leads to death while the other leads to life.

Personally, I've chosen life. I don't think I'll regret it.

seven

JESUS, THE LIGHT IN THE DARKNESS

"I am the light of the world. Whoever follows me will never walk in darkness, but will have the light of life."

JOHN 8:12

P eople who like to slither deep into the bowels of caves tell me that, when they extinguish their flashlights, the darkness is so deep you can actually feel it. Apparently, there are even caverns around the United States that offer guided tours where the attendant will turn off the house lights at some point during the tour. Folks who have paid good money to take one of these subterranean excursions (I am not one of those people) describe the overwhelming panic they first feel when they are plunged into total darkness.

Bill Huffman, a spokesman for a popular cave in Luray, Virginia, said, "'The darkness is disorienting, it can really affect your body. Constant pitch-black with no idea what direction you're moving can wear on you for sure.'"[1]

I don't recall ever being in darkness like that. There was a time or two, back in my more adventurous days, where I was deep in the woods in the middle of the night when the batteries on my not-so-trusty Maglite flashlight died. Navigating the swampy river bottoms of North Louisiana in almost total darkness is no fun, I can tell you. The best thing I can say is that until my eyes became somewhat acclimated to the faint moonlight and starlight, I had no idea what direction to take out of the woods.

There is perhaps nothing more frightening than being in an unfamiliar place and not being able to see your hand in front of your face. Total darkness can profoundly disorient us, and it isn't long before we are overcome with sheer panic.

Wherever I was lost on a dark night, my first option was to park my behind on the nearest log and wait for the first rays of daylight to pierce the tree branches above me. The other option, which never worked out well for me, was to simply pick a direction and head in it.

When lost in a dangerous place like that, neither choice seems appealing to me. Even during daylight hours, swamps can be dangerous. Deep water-filled holes and slithering reptiles that can either eat you whole or inject your flesh with toxic venom are always lurking nearby. At night, my mind conjured up images of what I had seen during the daylight.

Bob Newhart performed a skit several years ago where he played the part of a psychologist whose patient had an overwhelming fear of being buried alive in a box. She couldn't bear the thought of being engulfed in total darkness. Whether rational or not, the patient's fear of darkness was real to her, a debilitating fear that controlled almost every waking moment and kept her from sleeping at night. The only advice Newhart gave her every time she explained her fear was, "Stop it!"[2]

Well, if she could have just stopped it, I think she wouldn't have needed the psychologist. We are incapable of just stopping it when it comes to sin and the fear that accompanies spiritual darkness.

Most of us can certainly identify with Newhart's patient. We need light to illuminate familiar landmarks. Without light, we lose our bearings. We are lost, and there's not much more frightening than that. Bill Huffman was right—darkness is disorienting.

Spiritual Darkness

In 2015, I was invited to speak at the Conservative Political Action Committee (CPAC) in Washington, DC, where I received the Breitbart Defender of the First Amendment Award. I don't know what they expected, but I think I made them a little nervous when I pointed out that 110 million Americans carried a sexually transmitted disease in their bodies. "One out of three," I boomed in an overly dramatic voice.

One of the Robertson traits that sets us apart from normal folks is that we are experts at embellishing the stories we tell. Some of the younger bucks in my family now tell the story that I looked at the

CPAC crowd, motioned dramatically with my hand, and said, "Look to your right! Look to your left! One of you has an STD."

The problem with that story is, it never happened. I had one of the boys pull that speech up on YouTube just to do a fact-check on the Robertson boys, and I was relieved to find that they had made the whole thing up. Fake news!

Some of the people who traveled with me told me later that many in the crowd were applauding wildly, but there were a few who seemed to be squirming in their seats. I've never been known to be all that diplomatic, so it's possible I could have said the same thing in a different way.

Except what I said was true. The growing number of people with STDs is one piece of evidence that there is a spiritual darkness that has been creeping across our nation, and it's been coming on for a long time. The growing prevalence of sexually transmitted diseases is just one indicator. When mankind discards God's design for how we should live (including giving us a meaningful framework for our sexual expression), natural consequences follow.

What mankind has missed is that the entire Bible is an expression of God's plea to us, *No! No! Don't travel that path! It's dangerous! You're walking out of the light! You're walking into danger.*

Despite God's plan to keep us in his light, mankind has a habit of walking away from it into the dark and the murky moral swampland.

Israel is an example of a culture that made a habit of doing just this. Just before Moses died, he rallied the Israelites before him and gave them a final charge before they crossed the Jordan and took possession of the land that God had promised to give them. He was basically giving them the *Reader's Digest* version of their history after their exodus from Egypt.

As Moses recounted his encounter with God on the mountain when he received the Ten Commandments, he reminded the Jews how the darkness had stood as a barrier between them and God. They were doubtful people who had grumbled against the Lord (even though they had seen his miraculous intervention on their behalf), and because of this they were not permitted to be in God's presence. Their doubt in the goodness of God was their darkness. Only Moses was given permission to go behind the veil into God's physical presence.

> When you heard the voice out of the darkness, while the mountain was ablaze with fire, all the leaders of your tribes and your elders came to me. And you said, "The LORD our God has shown us his glory and his majesty, and we have heard his voice from the fire. Today we have seen that a person can live even if God speaks with them. But now, why should we die? This great fire will consume us, and we will die if we hear the voice of the LORD our God any longer." (Deut. 5:23–25)

This is the problem with spiritual darkness. It obscures the reality of the God who is not only there but is infinite in every way. Infinitely powerful! Infinitely present! Infinitely good! But when we choose darkness, it overshadows our view of the literal Creator of the cosmos.

When we choose darkness, it overshadows our view of the literal Creator of the cosmos.

The God Who Desires Us

Perhaps you've never thought of the Creator as a being who deeply longs to give you hope, but that is who the Bible says he is. When we do not choose him, we choose to live in darkness, where there is no hope. Our choice to avoid the light is a dangerous game, especially considering that the Light of the World has done everything he could do to convince us that he's on our side.

In the case of the Israelites, the darkness of their hearts clouded their vision of God too. Unfortunately, rather than listening to the loving God who was speaking to them, they completely misunderstood him and his desire for them. Rather than running to the voice of "his glory and his majesty," they fled from it. Their independent spirit of rebellion against God prevented them from seeing his goodness, while God, on the other hand, was always driven by one desire—*for them to come into his presence with a burning desire to be with him.*

> "Oh, that their hearts would be inclined to fear me and keep all my commands always, so that it might go well with them and their children forever!" (Deut. 5:29)

God only wanted one thing: for his people to fear and obey him, not because he was on some kind of narcissistic ego trip, but because he loved them, and he knew (better than they did) that if they walked with any other god beside him, they would be in the dark. As the only true sovereign God, he knew Israel would never be blessed in any other way. Everything outside of God's presence is darkness, and we will not find anything of value there. God knew that, so he pleaded with them and us to walk with him.

This was a cycle that Israel repeated generation after generation. God's desire was for his people to enjoy the generational blessing that naturally flows out of submission to the God who loved them. If you're looking for generational disaster, however, just follow the Israelites' recipe. But I warn you, it's a recipe for disaster.

1. They habitually left the God who loved them and walked into the darkness.
2. Their whole world came crashing down.
3. God would painfully discipline them until they returned to him and began walking in his light once more.
4. They repeated steps 1 through 3 over and over again for hundreds of years.

We must come to terms with one fact as we discuss our tendency to turn away from our loving Father. He hates it! It is disgusting to him! But the reason he finds our sin so revolting is not because we violated an external code of law; it is because when we turn away from him, we don't just reject his authority. When we do that, we are actually turning away from not just his law but from him.

Admittedly, our hearts can be hard toward God, but what if we could see him for who he really is? A loving father pleading with his children to come home. When we think about his true intentions for his creation in this way, we are left with three ugly options:

1. Either we hear his plea but don't care.
2. We don't see him as an infinite God who is beyond our ability to understand.
3. We can't see or hear him because we have traveled so far into the darkness that we are completely blind.

From our point of view as prideful human beings, it seems beneath God to plead with us to come to him. But I can't read the Scriptures any other way. So, I've concluded there is only one explanation for how mankind could turn away from God: we are coldhearted creatures hell-bent on self-reliance.

This is why God finds our refusal to trust his goodness so nauseating. We've turned our backs on a God who humbled himself to "death—even death on a cross" (Phil. 2:8).

The Revolting Nature of Rebellion

If you are questioning just how revolting our rebellion against God is to him, just ponder the following passage. And before you criticize me for including it in our discussion, just remember that I'm not the one who said it. I'm just quoting the Almighty.

Yet she became more and more promiscuous as she recalled the days of her youth, when she was a prostitute in Egypt. There she lusted after her lovers, whose genitals were like those of donkeys and whose emission was like that of horses. So you longed for the lewdness of your youth, when in Egypt your bosom was caressed and your young breasts fondled. (Ezek. 23:19–21)

In the most graphic language imaginable, God described how sickening the sin of the Jewish exiles in Babylon was to him. He compared them to a lover who no longer found joy in a monogamous relationship with her husband. Gone was the connection that is created when a husband and wife are in a sexual union and become one flesh. Gone was the tenderness and the community bond of two lovers who were deeply committed to one another. It was just about the raw sexual experience.

Perhaps this passage makes you uncomfortable, and it should. But the disturbing and graphic nature of this passage tells us exactly how God feels about the disgusting sin of mankind when we forsake the God who loves us and embrace the lies told by the Evil One and his minions instead.

If you are wondering how God views us when we walk in spiritual darkness, this is as plain as it gets.

Personally, I don't want to be like God's chosen people who ran away from the God who loved them. I don't want to inhabit the dark spiritual slums where the sunlight never shines. I have no desire to live where I am always looking over my shoulder and wondering what demonic being is setting me up for an ambush.

Instead, I want to live in the light, where my path is clearly illuminated and where I can see the obstacles that are in the middle of my route.

The Holy Spirit did not choose the word *darkness* lightly. It's a perfect word to describe a spiritual condition so bleak that it can only be understood as a complete absence of light. Without a light that comes from outside us, we become spiritually disoriented. We lose our moral bearings. When we are in darkness, the best we can do is grope around and blindly search for something that we can use to make sense of our lives. Unfortunately, we will never find it while we are turning a deaf ear to God.

That's a fact.

The reason that spiritual darkness is so debilitating to us is that, in our blind search for meaning, we tend to grab hold of things other than God to fill the void. That's the very definition of darkness. We're looking for something that will define us, to add meaning to our lives, but ironically, the only thing we can latch onto to attempt to find meaning is the very thing we are running from: God!

This is what the apostle Paul was talking about when he wrote:

> For you were once darkness, but now you are light in the Lord. Live as children of light (for the fruit of the light consists in all goodness, righteousness and truth) and find out what pleases the Lord. Have nothing to do with the fruitless deeds of darkness, but rather expose them. (Eph. 5:8–11)

In other words, spiritual darkness is our natural state. Universally, this is true across all cultures, genders, and nations. No human being can say that he has, by his own strength and power, escaped spiritual darkness. If you will notice, it isn't the specific sins that condemn us to the realm of darkness, but it is our rebellion against God. The deeds of darkness are "fruitless" because they are what we naturally gravitate toward when we aren't walking in the light. When we reject God, we turn to counterfeits that can only be described as the "fruitless deeds of darkness."

Paul listed a few of these fruitless dark deeds: sexual immorality, impurity, greed, obscenity, foolish talk, coarse joking, drunkenness, and debauchery (vv. 3–4, 18). There are other lists scattered throughout some of Paul's other letters as well, including idolatry, witchcraft, hatred, discord, jealousy, fits of rage, selfish ambition, envy, and homosexual behavior (Gal. 5:19–21; 1 Cor. 6:9–10; Rom. 1:28–32). These things are not the darkness itself, but they are behaviors that can only live in the darkness. The real darkness is when we do not enjoy the life of God.

So, lest we be tempted to think that the pathway to the Light is to pull ourselves up by our bootstraps and force ourselves to eliminate these things from our lives, I would like to point out what Paul said in the above passage: "You are light in the Lord" (v. 8)! Not just that you are *in* his light, but that you live in it, it lives in you, you share in it, and you reflect it. Jesus said that he is "the light of the world" (John 8:12). As light, he shines on us and his light is radiated by us to illuminate the darkness of the sin-cursed world.

In other words, we do not boot-strap ourselves by trying harder to be good. Instead, we are transformed by

When we walk with him, we learn to become more and more like him [God] every day, until we take our last breath.

walking with the Light of the World. When we walk with him, we learn to become more and more like him [God] every day, until we take our last breath.

This means that when Paul commanded us to "have nothing to do with the fruitless deeds of darkness, but rather expose them" (Eph. 5:11), he made two important points. First, avoid these behaviors like the plague, because they are indicators that you have wandered away from the Light. Don't flirt with them as if they are harmless. They are not! They are only trinkets, distractions that offer us freedom and purpose, but they actually suck the life and the light out of us with a goal of imprisoning us. They are designed by Satan and his henchmen to pull us away from what is really good, our Father in heaven (2 Tim. 2:26).

Second, when he instructed us to "expose" these fruitless deeds, he wasn't saying that we should expose them so we would feel the rush of power that comes from preaching hellfire and brimstone. Instead, he is pointing out the obvious, that these sins threaten our eternal existence. Why would we want to spend eternity with a God we've been rejecting our whole lives?

The list of sins from above are, indeed, indicators that we are in serious trouble. When we choose sin, we are questioning both God's wisdom and his goodness. And when we do that, we are building the same wall between God and us that stood between the Jews and God. In a very real sense, the devil's minions are screaming, "Build that wall!"

The Bible says, "Satan himself masquerades as an angel of light" (2 Cor. 11:14). This means that even though he promises light, he is actually luring us into rank spiritual darkness. Sadly, there are people who pose as pastors and teachers who are actually on the other team.

But I am the one responsible to God for my life. I am the one who must answer to him. No pastor, teacher, apostle, or church has ultimate authority over me. I am the one who has the responsibility to pray for wisdom and discernment as I study the Scriptures and search for God's purpose for my life.

This is why it is so important to be aware that there are people who hijack Jesus and use him to deceive those who are searching for the real Jesus. Paul said, "It is not surprising, then, if his [Satan's] servants also masquerade as servants of righteousness" (v. 15). So, I make it my goal to keep my eyes wide open, looking for the devil's next move. You never know where he is lurking or who he will employ to do his dirty business.

Being skeptical is not the same as being cynical. You might be surprised to hear me say that you should check out everything I tell you by looking at Scripture to see if I'm telling it right. Hey, don't trust me! I'm just a man!

> Now the Berean Jews were of more noble character than those in Thessalonica, for they received the message with great eagerness and examined the Scriptures every day to see if what Paul said was true. (Acts 17:11)

If God honored the Bereans for their skepticism, then why should you fail to fact-check your favorite pastor or teacher? And if you are a pastor, are you above this? Would it offend you if your congregation said, "We hear what you say, Preacher, but if you don't mind, we are going to go home and check it out for ourselves"?

The point is that if our desire is to "walk in the light, as he is in the light" (1 John 1:7), we cannot afford to allow anyone or anything to stand in our way. Not even the apostle Paul. Too much is at stake, because the greatest treasure that anyone could ever hope to have is one that will not rust or decay and that cannot be taken from us (Matt. 6:19–21). I don't want to miss out on that simply because I am too lazy to open my Bible and be my own fact-checker.

When I lived in the darkness, I saw the Light of the World as a threat to my own sovereignty. I realize now just how foolish I was. I was never a sovereign being; instead, I was under the control of the Evil One (1 John 5:19). At the precise moment in my life that I thought I was free, I was actually a slave, a prisoner, of Satan. Everyone living in darkness has been taken captive to do his will, and that was certainly true of me (2 Tim. 2:26; Rom. 6:16).

As it turns out, the Light of the World was never a threat to me at all. That's because his affection for me never wavered. When I was drunk, high, and sleeping around, he still loved me. I was in the valley of the shadow of death. My problem was, I didn't know I lived in darkness.

> "the people living in darkness
>   have seen a great light;
> on those living in the land of the shadow of death
>   a light has dawned." (Matt. 4:16)

Imagine that! When we lived in darkness, even though we didn't recognize it as darkness, God sent a brilliant light to shine on us and everything around us. I was dead in my trespasses and sins and in full-scale rebellion against God and his kingdom. Still, he sent me the Light of the World to show me the way.

The above passage from Matthew is actually quoted from Isaiah, who prophesied the coming of Jesus. In the ninth chapter of the prophet's book, the verse before the one Matthew quoted is this: "There will be no more gloom for those who were in distress" (v. 1).

Maybe you can't comprehend how joyfully and readily I welcomed the light once I finally heard the full story of Jesus, but saying that it suddenly dawned on me is an understatement. It was a new day, the first day of the rest of my life that I have lived since then. I walked out of the darkness, readily throwing off the "fruitless deeds of darkness," and have been walking in the light for the past almost fifty years. I don't regret a minute of it, because I now see that my life was fruitless before I met Jesus.

Think about it: I was stumbling around in the dark (literally), hiding from God and anyone I thought was on his side. Nothing good came out of my blind obedience to the spirit of disobedience (Eph. 2:2). I was rescued, for crying out loud. Why would I look upon that dark time in my life with any emotion other than disgust? The thought of returning to it sickens me.

> For he has rescued us from the dominion of darkness and brought us into the kingdom of the Son he loves, in whom we have redemption, the forgiveness of sins. (Col. 1:13–14)

In every way, I have been rescued from the kingdom of darkness and translated into God's kingdom, where I live, not in chaotic darkness, but in illuminating light.

I need to give you a little caveat here, a warning. Just because you are finished with the darkness, doesn't mean the darkness is finished with you. I make it my goal to please the Lord. In fact, I am obsessed with doing that. Still, I have that unspiritual part of my flesh where desire still lives.

No problem! God has a plan for that, too, which I found in these verses from 1 John:

> God is light; in him there is no darkness at all. If we claim to have fellowship with him and yet walk in the darkness, we lie and do not live out the truth. But if we walk in the light, as he is in the light, we have fellowship with one another, and the blood of Jesus, his Son, purifies us from all sin. (1:5–7)

> My dear children, I write this to you so that you will not sin. But if anybody does sin, we have an advocate with the Father—Jesus Christ, the Righteous One. He is the atoning sacrifice for our sins, and not only for ours but also for the sins of the whole world. (2:1–2)

So, yes, we are saved from the penalty of sin, and we are also saved from the control of sin. He moved us from where we once lived (darkness) to a new kingdom where he lives. We've changed locations and we've changed masters. We left Satan and now follow Jesus.

What this means is that our goal is to avoid sin like the plague that it is and imitate the Savior we live with and who lives in us.

So, yes, after all these years, I find myself falling down on the job once in a while. I take my eyes off of the light and look elsewhere, even if only for a brief moment. Pay attention to what John said here, though: the blood of Jesus still purifies me from all sin. I still have that defense attorney in Jesus, who advocates for me. He is still my atoning sacrifice.

This is why I follow the Light of the World. In spite of my best efforts to be like him, I am not 100 percent there yet. I want to be. I wish I were, but I'm not. But I'm still good to go because I follow him. He has my back in a way that is inconceivable to me, and I trust him that he's telling me the truth. I still walk with him because I believe in him.

When we walk in the light, we hate what the source of that light hates. We've already established that God hates sin, that it is disgusting to him, not because we violated an arbitrary code, but because sin reflects the exact opposite of God's nature. It is in direct opposition to what gives life. In fact, sin always leaves the stench of death in its wake.

This is, in part, the point that Jesus made when he said:

"I am the light of the world. Whoever follows me will not walk in darkness, but will have the light of life." (John 8:12)

The Light of the World isn't a concept or idea but a person. He became a human being when he descended to this planet and took on human flesh, but he was a person before then. In this sense, he is a personal God, not my private God who jumps up when I snap my fingers, but a personal God in that he is a real person.

He calls upon us to leave the darkness and follow him. The Bible uses the phrase "walk in the light" (1 John 1:5–7), but Jesus didn't say that here. Here, he said that if we follow him we will "have the light of life." In other words, when we follow him, he gives himself to us. He becomes our possession in a sense. But we also belong to him. We become his bride and he is our husband (Eph. 5:22–23; Rev. 19:7–9; 2 Cor. 11:2).

The bride of Christ is not yet perfect. But when we "have the light of life," we can walk in faithfulness. That's my goal! In the few remaining years I have left, I plan on continuing to walk faithfully with him. I may mess up along the way, but I can assure you of one thing: I will never go back into the darkness in which I once lived. That's a fact you can count on. I like living in the light too much to ever return.

eight

JESUS, THE RESURRECTED SIN OFFERING

"I have made you known to them, and will continue
to make you known in order that the love you have for
me may be in them and that I myself may be in them."

JOHN 17:26

As soon as I ran into Jesus, I left my old life. Just like that, I turned my back on my old way of doing things and the people I did it with. There was no hesitation about it, because, by that time, the weight of my sin was piled high on my shoulders. I was done with it. It was too heavy to carry around anymore.

As I said earlier, just because you're done with Satan, it doesn't mean he's done with you.

The truth of this became apparent to me not long after I was baptized. Miss Kay and I had scraped up enough down payment money to purchase the twenty-five-thousand-dollar house we live in to this day.

The only problem was, we didn't really have a solid plan about how we would make our mortgage payments, but I figured if I worked hard enough running nets in the river, I could catch enough fish to sell to the old man who ran the fish market in West Monroe to make it work.

So, until I got Duck Commander healthy enough to bring in enough money to feed my hungry family, I would get up early every morning and empty the hundred or so hoop nets I had strategically placed along the banks of the Ouachita River.

Channel cat! Buffalo carp! Gasper goo (the tasty freshwater drum)! And a few other species thrown in for good measure.

It was hard work, but it paid the bills—barely! At least we never went hungry. I didn't mind it, though, because I had a dream, even if no one else in this compassionate family of mine believed in my dream. Not long after I came up with my duck call idea, I walked into Ma and Pa's house, held up the prototype for my first call, and announced to the entire family, "This is going to make us rich!"

Old Pa looked up from his domino game, grunted, and mumbled, "Your play, Al."

Yes, I come from a long line of sensitive and supportive people.

However, I was not deterred. I may be as insensitive as the rest of the Robertsons, but I'm also just as stubborn. I just kept on plugging, making one duck call at a time, while running my nets on the river.

As I said, we got by, but looking back on it, the truth is, we were barely keeping our heads above water.

After a few months, I noticed something disturbing was happening far too regularly. Whenever I muscled my nets up from the murky water, I found that someone had beaten me to it. No fish! Just empty nets! Stealing my fish was bad enough, but in order to make a hasty exit before getting caught, the lazy scoundrels had sliced through the net webbing. Needless to say, this rendered my nets useless. They were worthless until I spent hours repairing them.

To say I was furious would be an understatement. Here I was, working like a dog to put a few groceries on my family's table, and these river rats were robbing me blind.

Remember, I wasn't long out of my previous life of sin and violence. I regret to report that the strategy I devised for catching the fish thief or thieves did not involve the Spirit of God.

I hid my jon boat on the opposite bank behind some overhanging cottonwood and button willow limbs and waited. It wasn't long before a couple of rough-looking characters came motoring by, looking up and down the river to see if anyone was watching. Then they slid their rig up to where one of my nets was tied up. I quietly watched them cut the webbing and dump the contents into their boat.

I waited until the crime had been consummated. Then I hit full throttle on my outboard and flew right up to their boat before they knew what was going on. I used a line I've been perfecting since boyhood: "Everyone's got a story, boys. What's yours?"

They stammered and stuttered a couple of seconds, when I noticed one of them was reaching for a pistol. What he didn't know is that I had my Browning 16-gauge loaded with five rounds of number-five buck-shot in my hand. Before he could make a move, I raised my shotgun and matter-of-factly told him, "Not a good idea, son! Not a good idea at all, unless you want to die today."

Occasionally stealing a few fish is one thing, but destroying my nets is another. We're talking about survival for me and my family. So, while I had them well covered with my shotgun, I demanded one thing from them.

"I'll be needing your driver's licenses, boys!"

They were prosecuted, and both lost their jobs with the fire department. They were even fined by the judge who found them guilty, but I didn't get a dime out of it. No restitution, no payback. Nothing!

I asked the judge, "Where do I go to get my money?" and his reply shook my already unstable faith in the criminal justice system.

"Oh, you'll have to take them to civil court for that."

I was shocked. I was the one who had been victimized by these young men, they got what they deserved, the court made money on it, and I went home empty-handed. I resolved that, from that day forward, I would take care of these matters on my own.

Thankfully, the Almighty saw me as a work in progress.

Not too long after this incident, I happened to motor up on another couple of young men emptying my nets. Like the first time, I slid up next to their boat and asked them what they were up to.

Same as before, they hemmed and hawed for a few seconds before I took control. But this time, the Holy Spirit was guiding my reaction to the thievery. I had just read a passage from Romans. It had been eating at my heart in the days leading up to this encounter.

Do not repay anyone evil for evil. Be careful to do what is right in the eyes of everyone. If it is possible, as far as it depends on you, live at peace with everyone. (Rom. 12:17–18)

You could argue with me about whether my first encounter with the fish-stealing rednecks reflected obedience on my part to this command, but after all these years, I'm thinking I probably didn't handle it in a godly manner.

I kept hearing "Do not repay anyone evil for evil" over and over again. No matter how hard I tried, I couldn't shake the feeling that I might have chosen a more godly response.

Just before I reached their boat, a thought hit me, one I had never had before.

"You boys must be gonna have a fish fry tonight," I said.

I had already emptied a few of my nets, so my boat was full of fish. They stammered and stuttered for a few seconds as I grabbed one fish after another and began to toss them into their boat. I could tell that my generosity was making them nervous because their butts began to squirm around on their boat's aluminum benches.

"Uh, that's enough, sir! We don't need any more!"

"Hah, you boys are gonna need more than this. I know how this operates. You fire up that peanut oil, slide a few battered slabs into it, and it always attracts rednecks. Nothing like the smell of frying fish to attract way more river rats than you anticipated."

Finally, I stopped, cocked my head to one side, and told them plainly, "I live right up there in that white house on the hill. If you boys ever need fish and can't catch enough or can't afford to buy them, just knock on my door and ask me. I'll take care of you. But don't steal them. The Almighty doesn't take kindly to thieving."

You may not believe it, but without the law getting involved, without any threats of violence, I never had another problem with anyone stealing my fish. Not once. I guess the word got around: "That redneck in the white house is crazy!"

Mercy Triumphs Over Judgment!

I learned a valuable lesson that day: mercy always triumphs over judgment! Did they steal? Yep! Were they guilty? Of course they were! But while the gospel had been planted in my heart when I ran into the first group of boys, it had only recently started to take root and sprout. God was still operating on me to ferret out any remaining vestiges of the old Phil.

However, when I caught the second couple of guys red-handed, the gospel had started to produce a little more of the fruit of the Spirit. What I had finally begun to grasp is that God had caught me in the act too. Those boys were no more guilty than I had been, and to some extent still was.

I am not going to rehash my past life here by giving you every sordid detail, because my former way of life when I was neck-deep in debauchery, dishonesty, and immorality is well documented. I'm not proud of what I did, but I've told my story a thousand times in the hopes that someone will hear how God saved me. I'm always hopeful that hearing that story will give someone else a glimmer of hope that God can redeem them too.

However, here's the bottom line of it all. I was guilty! As guilty as a man could be.

The debt I owed was my problem. How could a man as guilty as I was get anywhere near a god as holy as the God who created the universe? I knew that, as amazing as creation was, the God who made it was far more amazing than that. I knew he was incomprehensible in a way that made him unapproachable. He would never accept me, I was certain of that.

My unworthiness stood as a barrier between God and me. This barrier was real in my mind. It was of no comfort to me that all of mankind has this barrier in common with me. I just couldn't shake the feeling of separation, no matter how hard I tried.

The apostle Paul accurately described me:

Once you were alienated from God and were enemies in your minds because of your evil behavior. (Col. 1:21)

You could rightly argue that I viewed the boys who stole my fish as my enemies. That would certainly be true of the first group who destroyed the nets I used for feeding my family. But in another sense, they thought of themselves as my enemies, too, even though they'd never met me and didn't even know my name. Their own guilt caused them to see me differently. In a sense, they dehumanized me. That's why one of them reached for his pistol. If a man steals from or draws a gun on his fellow man, he must first reduce him to something less than human.

By the way, this is also the mechanism behind our rejection of God. Before we can get rid of him, we must reduce him to something less. In order to throw off what we consider to be his shackles, we must shrink him down to a god with a little *g*.

This has been Satan's strategy since the beginning—to convince mankind that God is something less than the all-powerful, majestic, holy being who freely creates matter out of nothing. He's a little-*g* god, unworthy of our worship and is, therefore, unworthy to sit on the throne he occupies. Satan convinces us that we could do a much better job at being God than the Almighty does. In essence, he convinces us to demand of God, "Move over and let me show you how it's done." It's not a difficult task for Satan, since that's what we want to hear anyhow.

This is the theme of the entire first chapter of Romans. Paul made the case in the first seventeen verses that only by worshiping Jesus can mankind be completely satisfied, not only in eternity, but in the here and now.

> I am not ashamed of the gospel, because it is the power of God that brings salvation to everyone who believes: first to the Jew, then to the Gentile. (v. 16)

The only way the barrier between God and me could be destroyed is for God to do something about it. I sure couldn't do anything. And according to Paul, this is what God did in Jesus. Someone had to pay for what I did, and lo and behold, that someone turned out to be the Creator of the world. What I could not accomplish—pay for my sin— the Son of God did when he shed his blood.

The story of Jesus is called *the gospel* because it is good news. That's what *gospel* means. In fact, I can't think of any news that's any better than this. Because he paid the debt I owed, I can now approach the Father with confidence (Heb. 4:16). The good news is that, through Jesus, he restores the big G to his name. We made him less, but he makes himself more!

What I could not accomplish— pay for my sin— the Son of God did when he shed his blood.

Even though God restored himself in my heart and treated me with kindness when I was at my worst, it was not how I treated the first group of thieves. I gave them what they deserved. I hammered them with the law.

Thankfully, after God worked on me a bit, I did a much better job of reflecting the nature of Jesus by the time I ran into the second group of thieves. Rather than giving them what they deserved, I gave them what they needed. Yes, I gave them the fish, but by the grace of God, I gave them some of the grace that I had been given. I was merciful. I gave them that because that's what they needed way more than they needed my fish.

By the time of the second incident, I had started to figure out that I could not afford to be less merciful to the man who owed me a few bucks than the God of the universe was to me by forgiving me of the millions I owed him (Matt. 18:21–35). In light of the Son of God shedding his blood for my worthless hide, what's a few catfish to a guy like me?

The Innocent for the Guilty

If you were to look at the murder of Jesus as nothing more than an unjust execution, you would miss the mystery of it. Crucifixion was such a brutal practice that the emperor Constantine put a stop to it in the fourth century. But before he did, thousands upon thousands died on Roman crosses over a five-hundred-year span. Most of those executions were unjust.

In the first century, execution by hanging on a cross was a practice in full swing. The eighteenth and nineteenth chapters of John's gospel give a detailed account of Jesus' murder. It was a brutal way to die, that's for sure, but it wasn't the brutality of it that made his death stand out from all of the other crucifixions of Jesus' day. Every one of them was brutal.

In order to find out why Jesus' execution was so different from all of the others who died on Roman crosses, we need to go back to the Old Testament to find our answer.

Very soon after Adam and Eve defied God and declared their independence from him, God strolled through the garden and called out their names. When he found them, they had sewn a few fig leaves together in a vain attempt to hide their exposed private parts. God could have said, *Good try, kids! I can still see your naked behinds!* Instead, he rebuked them and announced the sentence they would receive for distrusting him. He essentially said to them, *You've blown it! You could have lived forever, but no, you had to do it your way. Therefore, the natural consequence of your trying to play God is that, from now on, life will be hard for you—very hard. You'll scratch out a living from the dirt, childbirth will be very painful, and eventually you will die.*

158

There they were, caught in the act! Naked and afraid, hiding from God in the bushes!

Then God did something so profound that if you don't read closely, you will miss a hint of what his plan for our condition was.

The LORD God made garments of skin for Adam and his wife and clothed them. (Gen. 3:21)

Skins! I had read that verse a thousand times before it dawned on me. Where would God get skins to cover their nakedness? Then it hit me: God killed animals of some sort and skinned them to fashion something that would cover their shame.

This is the first sacrifice in the Bible. An innocent animal shedding its blood to cover the sins of the guilty. A sinless creature bleeding to cover the nakedness of sinners.

Over the next two thousand years, this ritual was repeated hundreds of thousands of times, maybe millions. When God gave Moses the Law, he provided a way for the Israelites to redeem themselves from their guilt, and that way always involved blood.

The LORD said to Moses, "Say to the Israelites: 'When anyone sins unintentionally and does what is forbidden in any of the LORD's commands—

"'If the anointed priest sins, bringing guilt on the people, he must bring to the LORD a young bull without defect as a sin offering for the sin he has committed. He is to present the bull at the entrance to the tent of meeting before the LORD. He is to lay his hand on its head and slaughter it there before the LORD. Then the anointed priest shall take some of the bull's blood and carry it into the tent of meeting. He is to dip his finger into the blood and sprinkle some of it seven times before the LORD, in front of the curtain of the sanctuary. The priest shall then put some of the blood on the horns of the altar of fragrant incense that is before the LORD in the tent of meeting. The rest of the bull's blood he shall pour out at the base of the altar of burnt offering at the entrance to the tent of meeting.'" (Lev. 4:1–7)

Time after time, year after year, century after century, and millennium after millennium, the innocent suffered for the guilty. On and on and on this practice continued until Jesus came along.

I'll admit that this was a rather gruesome practice. Some may even call it barbaric. One could even argue that it was unfair to make the innocent suffer for the guilty, and I would agree.

However, the practice of animal sacrifice branded the repulsive ugliness of sin into the minds of the Israelites. Every time a bull, heifer, goat, or dove was slaughtered, they were reminded that when we sin, blood must be spilled to pay for the crimes of the guilty.

Of course, animal sacrifice could never atone for sin. In fact, that was never God's purpose. He was only setting us up for the ultimate sacrifice:

The old system under the law of Moses was only a shadow, a dim preview of the good things to come, not the good things themselves. The sacrifices under that system were repeated again and again, year after year, but they were never able to provide perfect cleansing for those who came to worship. If they could have provided perfect cleansing, the sacrifices would have stopped, for the worshipers would have been purified once for all time, and their feelings of guilt would have disappeared.

But instead, those sacrifices actually reminded them of their sins year after year. For it is not possible for the blood of bulls and goats to take away sins. (Heb. 10:1–4 NLT)

The fur coats that God made for Adam and Eve did not change the fact that they were guilty. Nor did the blood of bulls and goats the Jews spilled in the temple really take away sin. They only pointed to a better and future sacrifice that really does wash away our guilt.

If you will take the time to read the rest of the tenth chapter of Hebrews, you'll find out just who that sacrifice was:

Under the old covenant, the priest stands and ministers before the altar day after day, offering the same sacrifices again and again, which can never take away sins. But our High Priest offered himself to God as a single sacrifice for sins, good for all time. Then he sat down in the place of honor at God's right hand. There he waits until his enemies are humbled and made a footstool under his feet. For by that one offering he forever made perfect those who are being made holy. (Heb. 10:11–14 NLT)

Think about it, a ritual performed hundreds of thousands of times made a permanent mark on the culture of the Jews. But was it enough in their minds? I don't know this for sure, but I am convinced the

Israelites were a lot like I would have been, asking themselves, *How can animal blood remove my sin?*

Perhaps this explains why they were so prone to do the wrong thing. In spite of the miracles God had performed in their presence, in spite of the gift of the promised land, and in spite of repeatedly being rescued from the consequences of their own sin, they were still drawn to the promises of prosperity made by false gods. They just weren't sure that God had forgiven them. They weren't confident that he would come through for them. Somehow, goat blood just didn't seem to do the trick. Only the blood of the Lamb of God would. But they didn't know that yet.

The lesson we should learn from this is that unwashed sin is a burden that will destroy anyone who tries to carry it. It destroyed the Jews more than once. It destroys us too. And when a nation turns from God and begins to worship created things instead of the Creator, it will also be destroyed.

> They exchanged the truth about God for a lie, and worshiped and served created things rather than the Creator—who is forever praised. Amen. (Rom. 1:25)

The Final Sacrifice

But in Jesus, God has given us something more enduring, more secure. For sure, it's far better than living a life of destruction. The gift that God has given to mankind is that he sacrificed himself as an offering for our sin. For centuries, the innocent died for the guilty, but it really didn't do much to make us feel clean; it only made us more aware of our sin.

Now, the perfect sacrifice, the sinless, holy God who created the universe offered himself as a blood sacrifice. No more bulls and goats. God put himself on the altar as the final offering.

Whew! Finally, mankind can take a deep breath and relax, not by taking sin lightly, but by resting in the security that everything is, once and for all, taken care of. Finally, the guilt and shame of our sin is eradicated and we can return to the Garden of Eden where we can walk with God without shame. Finally, we are clothed with Christ so completely that when he looks at us, all he sees is Jesus.

> So in Christ Jesus you are all children of God through faith, for all
> of you who were baptized into Christ have clothed yourselves with
> Christ. (Gal. 3:26–27)

It's baptism into the sacrificed and risen Christ that makes us right. Not just water baptism, but immersion into the person of Jesus. Not simply being dunked in water, but putting Jesus on as a garment.

This is why I harp on water baptism so much. It symbolizes being completely covered by Jesus and his blood. Water baptism isn't the real thing any more than the bread and wine of the Lord's Supper are the literal blood and flesh of Christ. But saying that communion and baptism are symbolic of a greater truth isn't to say they are unimportant.

I've had a few famous theologians rake me over the coals on social media for my views on baptism (even though they never bothered to call me to find out what my views are). But if you want to argue about baptism, all I'll ask you is why would a man want to discourage someone from participating in something with such rich symbolism? I never point to myself and say, "The water saved me!" But I do point to the day of my immersion in water as the day that I began a new life.

That's because when I found out Jesus had paid for my stinking sins and that I could do something symbolic that mimics what he did, I jumped at the chance. I wanted in on his grace. Since I was worn out from my sin, I heard what the pastor read to me from Scripture, that I needed to turn my back on my sins, put to death and bury the old Phil, and be raised up to walk a new life (Rom. 6:1–4).

As I said, I didn't hesitate. Like the Ethiopian eunuch told Philip, "Baptize me right now! Why wait?" (Acts 8:36). I was ready to begin my new life right on the spot.

Baptism is a physical connection to the reality that when we latch onto the crucified Lord Jesus, he covers us, surrounds us, wraps around us like a garment. As I said, the water of baptism wasn't the real thing, but I sure got the connection of the symbolism. I knew right off the bat that I was one with Jesus Christ. I was immersed in him, and that immersion cleansed me.

The Sacrifice Lives!

Having said all of this about Jesus being our sin offering, it wouldn't have really meant much if the Romans had hung him on a cross, buried him in a tomb, and left his body to rot. If that's the end of the story, how would we know whether or not his death truly had the power to remove our sins? Only a God powerful enough to raise a man from the dead would be powerful enough to pay for all the rotten, filthy things I've done. If you're like me, even though you may not admit it or even think about it much, the depth and permanence of your guilt sometimes keeps you awake in the quiet of the night.

Whether or not it torments you, I'll tell you this about me: I knew I was guilty and there was nothing I could do to make up for it. My sense of powerlessness to do anything about my guilt was crippling.

So, when I heard that God had provided a way to purify me from my sins, I was stunned. But I thought to myself, *How can I know for sure?* Therefore, when I read the Gospel accounts of Jesus' resurrection from the dead, I cried out, "That's it! That's how I know! God raised my sin offering from the dead!"

This was my rationale for jumping into my new faith with both feet. As I've already freely admitted, I was not immediately perfect (just ask the fish thieves I pulled a shotgun on), and I am not perfect in my performance fifty years after the fact (just ask Miss Kay), but in the eyes of God I am perfect! Sinless! This is the result of believing in and trusting the risen Lord Jesus. My performance isn't good enough to cleanse me, that's for sure. But the performance of Jesus is.

> *Only a God powerful enough to raise a man from the dead would be powerful enough to pay for all the rotten, filthy things I've done.*

The result of my trusting the sacrifice of Christ and his resurrection from the dead is that I am in a contract of sorts with God. The only thing I am required to do is to believe him—that he's telling the truth about the death and resurrection of Christ—and follow Jesus. In return, he gives me freedom.

I'm now free from the control and penalty of sin! I'm free from guilt! I'm free from the law! I don't have to be perfect anymore! And I'm free from the grave! I'll be raised from the six-foot hole they will put me in when I die!

When I heard that, I said out loud, "Uh, that would be a home run!"

The practical meaning of all of this is that I am now free to approach God with confidence.

> So then, since we have a great High Priest who has entered heaven, Jesus the Son of God, let us hold firmly to what we believe. This High Priest of ours understands our weaknesses, for he faced all of the same testings we do, yet he did not sin. So let us come boldly to the throne of our gracious God. There we will receive his mercy, and we will find grace to help us when we need it most. (Heb. 4:14–16 NLT)

As I said, if it were left up to me and my performance, I could never confidently go anywhere near the holy and infinite God. If I went to him at all, I would go cowering and trembling with fear, crawling on my hands and knees due to my overwhelming personal guilt. But even if I could go to him, I wouldn't be able to stay there too long. Not before this God who is powerful enough to burn me to a crisp with a single word. I would have to make a hasty and rapid departure.

The truth is, no sinner can stand before the Almighty. Yet, in spite of God's seeming unapproachability, he invites us to come to him. But how? I am too sinful and he is too holy.

I've Heard Good News Before, But This . . .

And this is where the good news takes a sledgehammer to the barrier between us and God, the wall that was built by our sin. Instead of approaching him by calling attention to my nonexistent merits, I now go to him and point to the merit of Jesus who sacrificed himself for me. Read the passage above again. This is what we have in Christ:

- We have a great high priest (Jesus) who offered one sacrifice for our sins.
- That high priest is the sacrifice.
- Because he became one of us and was tempted in the same way we are, we can now be confident that he knows the depth of our suffering.
- He has ascended to heaven to sit at God's right hand, and from there he declares us sinless because we believe in him.

I tend to repeat myself, and one thing I always ask folks who hear me preach the name of Jesus is, "Do you have a better story? If so, I'd like to hear it!" What about you? Do you have a better story?

Over and over again, as we read the Bible, we hear the same story. Man is sinful and unable to approach God! Jesus, however, is good and purifies sinners from their guilt. He now sits at the Father's right hand and intercedes for us.

It was good news when the US Patent Office approved my first duck call patent. It was good news when I heard I could get a loan to purchase the equipment I needed to manufacture duck calls. It was also good news when we signed a contract to appear on *Duck Dynasty*.

But all of those things seem like nothing compared to hearing the good news that the God of heaven became a substitutional sacrifice for my sin. I will never hear better news than that.

nine

JESUS, THE RESTORER OF THE DEFEATED

"Simon, son of John, do you love me more than these?"

JOHN 21:15

F ool me once, shame on you; fool me twice, shame on me! In other words, "I don't put up with those who deceive me. I don't believe in second chances!"

This is how the world operates. We see it in politics and on social media. Late-night talk shows pile on those who've made mistakes. Take a wrong step or have a dispute with someone, and you quickly go on their do-not-call list.

This is mankind's default position. We don't tolerate betrayal or deceit or failure. Not at all!

But then along came Jesus! And when he came, he brought a new philosophy with him, one that was revolutionary and countercultural. His way of viewing mankind was the polar opposite of how we view others. And he turned the world upside down because of it.

The unique character and nature of Jesus is seen throughout the Gospels of Matthew, Mark, Luke, and John, and that's the theme of this book. I have been talking about a man who perfectly reflected the nature of God. And because he was different from all other men, we often find him doing the opposite of what all men do. Time after time he went off the beaten path to find and restore those defeated by sin. Most of us ignore the marginalized, but not Jesus! He went out of his way to find people who were disappointed with the consequences of their sin, even though sin is always ultimately an offense against Jesus.

Imagine that, the offended restoring the offenders. Go figure!

Yes, Jesus is different from me in all kinds of ways. But he's most different from me in the way that he reacted to those who mistreated him. I tend to want vengeance, while he always dispenses mercy.

One of the most appalling acts of betrayal against Jesus is found in the latter part of the Gospel of John. On the worst day of Jesus' life, after he had been seized and taken before the kangaroo court that was held in the temple of God, Peter denied he even knew Jesus. Not once, not twice, but three times!

Let's take a minute to review what led up to this betrayal by Peter. Jesus had been taken captive by the Jewish leaders and run through a mock trial. These men who pretended to be God's spokesmen didn't know or care about "innocent until proven guilty." Their goal was not to discover the truth about Jesus; they only wanted him dead. The trial was a pretext for murdering him. These allegedly good and religious men knew ahead of time what they were going to do with him; they just needed it to all be wrapped up in a neat little legal package. Like any good lawyer would do, they found a loophole in the law that allowed them to do what they wanted to do all along.

But long before they knew what they were going to do, Jesus knew. He knew before he came in the flesh. He came knowing the Pharisees would kill him and that Peter would deny him. Still, he came in spite of what he knew would happen to him.

And there was Peter bravely hanging in the shadows on the fringe of the angry crowd, following Jesus and the mob right up to the courtyard of the temple. We tend to give him a hard time because he denied he was a follower of Jesus, but I give him credit for at least not abandoning the Lord after the others had already scattered.

Finally, however, Peter caved in. Confronted with claims that he was a companion of Jesus, three times Peter denied he knew the Lord.

"I swear! I don't even know the man!"

Then, *cock-a-doodle-doo*! One lone sound from one of the dumbest animals on the planet, and Peter's world came crashing down around him. No one else would have given this hotheaded fisherman another shot. No one except Jesus. Jesus had seen potential in Peter when no one else had. And now? When it mattered most, he let Jesus down.

Before the rooster crowed, hours before Jesus' arrest, Peter had sworn he would die with Jesus. "Don't worry, Jesus! I have your back!"

Instead of thanking Peter for his support, the Lord rammed a dagger into Peter's heart. "You will deny me three times before the rooster crows" (John 13:38 CEB). Ouch! That had to hurt!

In spite of Peter's bravado, it happened just as Jesus said it would. The crowing of the rooster! Like a ton of bricks, it hit him. In a split second, he realized he had done what he swore he wouldn't do. The Bible records, "He went outside and wept bitterly" (Matt. 26:75; Luke 22:62).

Peter left the scene with his tail dragging between his legs. Defeated by his sin! He had just betrayed the one man he loved the most and who loved him the most.

He was right! I did what I thought I would never do! Oh, God!

Think about it! Peter had witnessed most of the miracles of Jesus. He had heard Jesus plainly tell them that he would die and be raised from the dead. Jesus was his friend.

But after all that, he still cowered in the shadows, trying to limit his contact with the one he had betrayed. His heart was weighed down with shame. He had crossed a line that couldn't be uncrossed. His sin was so profound he could not get over it. As far as Peter was concerned, this was as bad as it could get.

So, he told his friends he was going to return to what he was doing when Jesus called him—"'I'm going out to fish!'" (John 21:3). Time for a career change again.

Defeated, with no hope of recovery. *How does one get themselves out of a hole like this? It's too deep, and I'm too weak!*

We like to think we would have been different. If we had seen what Peter saw during the three years he did ministry with Jesus, we would have walked right into the courtroom and demanded they release Jesus from custody, right? Maybe! But I'm afraid I would have denied him too.

Thank God he doesn't operate by that old proverb of "Fool me once, shame on you; fool me twice, shame on me." Instead, Jesus went out of his way to restore his defeated friend. It's not that Jesus was fooled by Peter or the rest of the disciples. Jesus' willingness to give people second chances doesn't come from being naive. As I said, Jesus knew exactly what was going to happen. Just before he was nabbed by the mob, he told them in advance that they would all betray him:

> *Jesus' willingness to give people second chances doesn't come from being naive.*

> Then Jesus told them, "This very night you will all fall away on account of me, for it is written:

> > 'I will strike the shepherd,
> > And the sheep of the flock will be scattered.'" (Matt. 26:31)

Remember, it was Peter who rebuked the Lord for saying such a thing: "Even if all fall away on account of you, I never will" (v. 33).

"I have your back, Jesus!" Except he didn't. His bravery soon evaporated into thin air, and when the rubber met the road, he became the opposite of what he had promised Jesus he would be. Just like the rest of them, Peter, too, was now a deserter. In fact, he was more than a deserter, because he publicly denied him, vehemently denied him, with cursing, no less. He was a traitor!

But Jesus, who often went out of his way to keep his divine

appointments with unlikely prospects for citizenship in his kingdom, went out of his way to meet Peter in his hiding place on the beach.

Three years earlier, Jesus had called to Peter from the beach: "Come, follow me . . . and I will send you out to fish for people" (Matt 4:19). When Peter thought he had destroyed his relationship with Jesus, he returned to his old life. *Back to old strategies! Back to what I'm comfortable with. I'll just stick with what I'm good at. I'll go back to fishing for a living.*

Peter didn't remember it, but fishing is precisely what Jesus had in mind for Peter from the beginning. Peter's betrayal of Jesus had not changed a thing. Peter must have forgotten what Jesus told him when he first commanded him to leave his nets three years earlier:

> One day as Jesus was walking along the shore of the Sea of Galilee, he saw two brothers—Simon, also called Peter, and Andrew—throwing a net into the water, for they fished for a living. Jesus called out to them, "Come, follow me, and I will show you how to fish for people!" And they left their nets at once and followed him. (Matt. 4:18–20 NLT)

So Jesus sought Peter out to refocus him on his calling, to fish for men. With a few of the fresh-caught fish Jesus had filled their nets with, he touched Peter's broken heart and let him know that he still had bigger fish to fry. His denial of Jesus didn't change a thing; Peter was still a fisher of men. His sin didn't cancel his calling.

Who is Jesus? He is a holy, perfect, sinless, infinite, star-breathing, galaxy-hurling, universe-creating God who pays attention to traitors such as Peter. He is a God of incredible, unbelievable mercy and grace, who was willing to die to forgive the unforgivable. He purposely chose a band of misfit losers and transformed them into world changers, men who would lead people out of hopelessness and into hope. He came for them, he came for me, and he came for you.

I'm only telling you this because Satan would have us believe a different version of Jesus, one based on human constructs. His Jesus is a lot like you and me, the kind of person who says, "Fool me once, shame on you; fool me twice, shame on me!" With Satan's version of Jesus, second chances are hard to come by. Satan wants you to believe your identity is found in your screw-ups, because your mistakes are carved in stone and cannot be erased.

Sadly, there are more than enough Christians who freely cling to the Evil One's version of Jesus. This plays out in one of two ways. They are manifested as either Pharisaic legalists or church members who exist without joy or purpose. They are the defeated ones who hang their heads in shame, because they don't really know the Jesus revealed in the Gospels.

I don't have much to say that would encourage the pharisees among us, but to the defeated, I beg you to take a hard look at Peter's restoration. If anyone had reason to throw in the towel, it was him. In fact, that's precisely what he did. In his estimation, it was game over. *After what I did, there's no coming back!*

However, in Jesus, we find a man who is on the prowl, looking for defeated people who yearn for something better. Their guilt and shame had overwhelmed them, and they don't know how to shuck them off. In their minds, they are over the limit when it comes to their sin quota.

I find it interesting that Jesus never once said, "Okay! You've done it now! There's no coming back for you!" As a matter of fact, Jesus specializes in changing lives and turning traitors into patriots who love and long for his kingdom.

Just like he did for his friend Peter!

Did it work? Did his restoration of Peter make a difference?

All I can tell you is to take a little time and read the book of Acts. Only a month or so after Peter's betrayal of Jesus, this Christ denier was found standing before the same bunch that had crucified Jesus, preaching freedom from the defeat that sin brings to all men.

> "Fellow Israelites, listen to this: Jesus of Nazareth was a man accredited by God to you by miracles, wonders and signs, which God did among you through him, as you yourselves know. This man was handed over to you by God's deliberate plan and foreknowledge; and you, with the help of wicked men, put him to death by nailing him to the cross. But God raised him from the dead, freeing him from the agony of death, because it was impossible for death to keep its hold on him." (Acts 2:22–24)

What a transformation! What a restoration! A once-defeated man who had cowered before Jesus' murderers was now filled with incredible boldness, preaching the same name he had denied. And it all began on a beach with not a rooster in sight. The voice of shame was silenced by the resurrected Son of God.

Too far gone for God? Too far over the sin quota? Unredeemable?

That kind of thinking is demonic. It is rooted in our own sinful nature that finds it hard to give other people second chances. Peter was a lot like us. We are too often ready to throw in the towel after we sin, because we ourselves struggle with forgiving others. We aren't all that forgiving, so it's hard to imagine a God who is.

At one point during Peter's training, he tried to impress Jesus by suggesting that the bag limit on forgiving others was as high as seven times.

"Lord, how many times shall I forgive my brother or sister who sins against me? Up to seven times?" (Matt. 18:21)

In Peter's mind, he was being generous. I mean, who forgives someone seven times? After all, "Fool me once, shame on you; fool me twice, shame on me." And here he was, putting his best foot forward, stretching the limit all the way out to seven.

I bet Jesus will be impressed with me now!

But Jesus had a different perspective on forgiveness than Peter did.

Jesus said to him, "I do not say to you, up to seven times, but up to seventy times seven." (v. 22 NKJV)

Now, let's see, seventy times seven? Seven times zero is zero. Seven times seven is forty-nine. *Four hundred ninety times!* You have to be kidding me! No one can forgive like that!

That's a lot of forgiving. No one could forgive one person that much—except Jesus and those who have been forgiven by a sovereign and holy God. That's the point! Jesus was calling on Peter to become like him. To see the power of unlimited grace. To forgive as he forgave

Peter. And to restore all the lonely and defeated people in the same way Peter had been restored by Jesus.

This concept is not only revolutionary, it is liberating like no other thought can liberate. To forgive as God forgives and dispense mercy as freely as Jesus does? Now that's as life-changing as it gets!

The other way, the way of limited mercy? It's crippling. Living under a system like that is wearisome. It is a burden too great for any human to carry. It will wear you out and compel you to give up. It is unattainable and unsustainable. No man, no woman, no child can live under the weight of crushing guilt and shame. Sooner or later, we all give up and return to our own version of fishing. Even old, failed strategies for dealing with our sin look more appealing than the crushing burden of believing that God hates us.

Back to the alcohol! To the drugs! To the practice of heartless religion! To materialism and consumerism! Back to what we did before we tried this Jesus thing. Back to anything that will keep us from remembering how badly we have blown it.

Talk about a burden! It's completely unsustainable. It's like living under a microscope where all of our sins and failures are magnified and put on display on the worldwide web for all to see.

Even though I once tried to carry this burden myself, I do so no longer. It's not that I'm superior to you or anyone else. Instead, I found someone stronger to carry my burdens and restore me to sanity. Remember the verse we talked about earlier in chapter three?

"Come to me, all you who are weary and burdened, and I will give you rest. Take my yoke upon you and learn from me, for I am gentle and humble in heart, and you will find rest for your souls. For my yoke is easy and my burden is light." (Matt. 11:28–30)

I will never find rest in my old strategies, but only in coming to Jesus. Not the systems of religion or a code of law, but in coming to a person, to Jesus.

As I've said before, continuing to live in defeat is insanity, but we can't just bootstrap ourselves out of it. There's no pill, no mental health therapy that can restore order to our lives. According to Jesus himself, we can only experience healing by coming to him with our weariness and our burdens.

However, we need to know one thing about what it takes to get in on the rest that God offers. Restoration is only available to those who have, like Peter, come to the end of themselves and admitted they've really blown it. It is not for the proud or the ones who think they just need a little help.

If anyone wants in on this kind of restoration, the path is simple.

- Take a hard look at yourself.
- Take an honest moral inventory of your life.
- Look at your hands and determine what thing of value you have to offer Jesus in exchange for his death on your behalf.
- Once you realize that your hands are empty, bow before his cross, admit your worthlessness, and plead with him to restore you.

Once you've done that, you are in a position of humility, and a humble person is the only person ready for Jesus to take them by the hand and lift them to their feet.

I find it interesting that Peter, a man who failed so miserably, could write the following years later, after his appointment with Jesus on the beach:

> "God opposes the proud
>   but shows favor to the humble."

> Humble yourselves, therefore, under God's mighty hand, that he may lift you up in due time. Cast all your anxiety on him because he cares for you. (1 Peter 5:5–7)

It's not just that we need to humble ourselves, but that we humble ourselves under "God's mighty hand." Our hands are empty, but his mighty hand is full of grace and truth. Only his hand is capable of lifting us up to live, not in defeat, but in victory, a victorious life that is freely given to us in spite of our failure to keep his law.

If you want to know the source of our anxiety, this is it. When we take a look at the worthless trinkets in our own hands and realize they have no value before God, we fall into despair. We know we have blown it and can do nothing to make things right with God. The truth is, if we keep looking at our own hands, we will only find that we are more anxious about not only our present circumstances but our eternal future. Deep down inside of us, we know we can't do a single thing to change our destiny.

But Jesus pleads with us to come to him. The Holy Spirit makes a similar plea, "Cast all your anxiety [cares] on him" (v. 7). This is humility, to recognize that we are unable to bear the weight of our own anxiety.

It is only when we gather it all up in one huge pile and simply throw it in God's lap we can really be free of it. We can be sure of one thing: a God who can create a universe is big enough to handle our cares. With room to spare.

If you're wondering why a God so big and mighty would go to the trouble of inviting you to dump it all in his lap, the passage quoted above tells you why. It's because he cares for you. As hard as it is to believe a God like that would want anything to do with sinners like you and me, it is true, nonetheless. He cares for me! He cares for you!

But why does he love us? It's because he has made you and me in his image and has therefore made us the objects of his affection. Why would he want to destroy his image bearers, for crying out loud? Destruction is what we choose when we reject him. He, on the other hand, chooses to pay for our restoration out of his own pocket.

Remember, Jesus' mercy is limitless. You don't have a sin quota. I'm not talking about the person who says, "Well, since I've been saved by grace, I can do what I want!" As a reminder, at least twice Paul condemned such thinking (Rom. 3:8, 6:1–2). He pegged that kind of thinking as demonic.

Instead, I'm talking about the dude who humbled himself under God's mighty hand and was lifted up, only to fall down again. I'm talking about the woman who finds herself in another promiscuous relationship and hates it. Or the young teenager who just can't seem to stop looking at porn, or the drug addict who can't find the strength to stop using.

Remember, Jesus' mercy is limitless. You don't have a sin quota.

To those people I say, humble yourself under God's mighty hand. Don't give up. Instead, be lifted up. Giving up is what you do. God, on the other hand, does not give up. He lifts up! And when we are lifted up by God, we are restored. One hundred percent fully restored, with no gaps!

As my friend Mac Owen tells his fellow Celebrate Recovery celebrants, "Keep coming back!" What he means is that giving up leads to hopelessness, but when we keep coming back to a community where God's restoration is celebrated, we find healing.

Keep coming back to Jesus. When you fall down, get back up and run to the only one who can restore you and rescue you from defeat.

Just like he did for Peter.

CONCLUSION

So, what's your point, Phil?

My point is this: if you are living in a fear that is driven either by shame and guilt or the increasing wickedness we all see unfolding in the world, I want to suggest that there is only one being in the universe who can restore order to your chaos. He claims he is the only one who is qualified to take our shame, guilt, and fear and transform us into victorious disciples who follow him into eternity.

This book touches on only a few of the qualifications that could be listed on Jesus' résumé. I simply can't cover them all. Here's a longer list. Who knows, maybe there's enough material for another book in the future, if God permits.

Jesus is all of the following:

- the Creator of everything
- sinless, never made a mistake
- miracle worker
- Alpha and Omega
- omniscient

- omnipresent
- omnipotent
- the way
- the truth
- the life
- the resurrection
- the Redeemer for everyone
- King over heaven and earth
- indestructible
- prophet
- mind reader
- Lawgiver
- judge
- the supreme being on heaven and earth
- ultimate love
- the man of mystery
- the great mediator of the saints
- the greatest defense attorney of all time
- conqueror of death
- full of grace
- full of mercy
- the greatest teacher
- Bread of Life
- the greatest healer
- reconciler
- fullness of God
- the greatest servant

- Lord of all
- high priest
- our seal
- greatest sacrifice
- unable to lie
- our escape hatch into eternity
- the great I Aᴍ
- the greatest intercessor
- author of our salvation
- the Son of God
- Savior
- the Light of the World
- in authority over Satan
- head of the church
- liberator from sin
- peacemaker between us and the Father
- greatest friend we could ever have

This is only a partial list of the attributes we could list on Jesus' résumé. However, there's enough here to at least pique a person's interest if they are looking for something or someone more substantive than the human constructs that fuel most people's view of how they should live their lives.

I've said it before, but I'll repeat myself here. I'm not arguing that anyone should follow Jesus just because he has a better story (even though he does). Instead, I am trying to prompt others to at least give his claim to be the divine Son of God a quick look. If it turns out that his claims of divinity are bogus, you haven't lost a thing, other than a few hours of Bible study. However, if he is who he claims to be, you will have discovered the portal into the throne room of God.

This means that if it turns out the Bible accurately represents Jesus, there's a lot at stake here. All I'm asking you to do is to give it a once-over. If you find out the whole story is phony, no harm done.

However, I do want to remind us all of one very important fact: *every human being worships something.* In Matthew 4:10, Satan tried to convince Jesus that he could give him something if Jesus would only bow down and worship him. The Evil One is pretty slick, but next to the Son of God, he comes across as being a little on the slow side, if you know what I mean. Jesus already owned it all, for crying out loud.

In response to Satan's illogical attempt to tempt him, Jesus quoted the Bible.

"It is written: 'Worship the Lord your God, and serve him only.'" (Matt. 4:10)

His weak efforts to tempt Jesus by offering him something else to worship besides God didn't work with the Lord, but the rest of us fall for it easily enough. In fact, when I look at my own life and the lives of almost everyone I know, it looks like our tendency is to worship anything we can find, other than God.

The word *worship*, according to my friend Webster, means to express adoration toward a deity.[1] That's one definition. But the word the Bible uses for worship in the passage above means "to make obeisance, do reverence to." Another way of saying this is, What we bow down to, what we obsess about, those are the objects of our worship.

Paul said that when we don't think it is worthwhile to worship God, we wind up worshiping created things instead (Rom. 1). And to tell the truth, it is one or the other, because we are compelled to worship. It's almost as if it's in our DNA to revere something, and in the absence of a desire to worship an infinite God, we will bow down before something or someone else.

In my opinion, this explains why we are so obsessed with things that won't last until the water gets hot. In case you aren't familiar with that idiom, just put a pot of water on the stove and bring it to a boil. The time between turning on the burner and when you see the water begin to dance around in the pot is relatively brief.

If you can grasp the concept of brevity, you can understand the futility of worshiping any physical object or even another member of the animal kingdom, including human beings. Neither physical objects nor humans last until the water gets hot. Everything either wears out or dies. No exceptions.

While we are all, by nature, consumers, in the end, we will be consumed by death. As I said in the introduction, without an infinite God providing definition to our existence, we are all just carbon. Jesus essentially said, however, "You are more than carbon to me, and I'll prove it by dying for your sins."

I looked at the list of Jesus' qualifications I listed above, and I wondered, *What if he's real? What if he really is that magnificent?* After years of looking him over, I have concluded that he is that wonderful. He really can replace my disappointment with the fading things of this world with a hope in "an eternal glory that far outweighs them all" (2 Cor. 4:17).

NOTES

CHAPTER 1: JESUS, THE CREATOR

1. "Pontiac GTO Judge Ram Air IV Specs," FastestLaps.com, 2003, https://fastesstlaps.com/models/pontiac-gto-judge-ram-air-iv-1969.
2. Friedrich Nietzsche, *The Gay Science: With a Prelude in Rhymes and an Appendix of Songs*, trans. Walter Kaufmann (1882; repr., New York: Vintage Books, 1974), 181.
3. Julia Mueller, "Record Percentage Says US Headed in Wrong Direction: NBC poll," The Hill, August 21, 2022, https://thehill.com/homenews/administration/3609791-record-percentage-says-us-headed-in-wrong-direction-nbc-poll/.
4. Vicky Stein, "What Is the Speed of Light?" Space, May 17, 2023, https://www.space.com/15830-light-speed.html.
5. Amanda Barnett, "Beyond Our Solar System," Solar System Exploration, April 20, 2023, https://science.nasa.gov/solar-system/.
6. Ailsa Harvey and Elizabeth Howell, "How many galaxies are there?" Space, February 1, 2022, https://www.space.com/25303-how-many-galaxies-are-in-the-universe.html; see also "How Many Galaxies are there in the Universe," The Nine Planets, September 29, 2020, https://nineplanets.org/questions/how-many-galaxies-are-there-in-the-universe/.
7. C. S. Lewis, *The Lion, the Witch, and the Wardrobe* (New York: Collier Books, 1950), 75–76.

CHAPTER 2: JESUS, THE KING OF KINGS

1. Joseph Goldstein and Joshua Needelman, "Fentanyl Helps Push Overdose Deaths to Record Level in New York City," *New York Times*, January 13, 2023, https://www.nytimes.com/2023/01/13/nyregion/new-york-overdose-record.html.

2. Sri Taylor, "Suicide Rates Resume US Rise After Two Years of Decline, CDC Report Says," Bloomberg, September 30, 2022, https://www.bloomberg.com/news/articles/2022-09-30/suicide-rates-resume-us-rise-after-two-years-of-decline-cdc-report-says.

3. "Ukraine War: US Estimates 200,000 Military Casualties on All Sides," BBC, November 10, 2022, https://www.bbc.com/news/world-europe-63580372.

4. Thomas Abt, Eddie Bocanegra, and Emada Tingirides, "Violent Crime in the U.S. Is Surging. But We Know What to Do About It," *Time*, January 12, 2022, https://time.com/6138650/violent-crime-us-surging-what-to-do/.

5. "The Trail of Tears," 1942, PBS, n.d., https://www.pbs.org/wgbh/aia/part4/4h1567.html.

6. "Abortion Statistics: United States Data and Trends," National Right to Life Educational Foundation, January 2022, https://nrlc.org/uploads/factsheets/FS01AbortionintheUS.pdf.

7. Helen Howarth Lemmel, "Turn Your Eyes Upon Jesus," 1922, Hymnary, https://hymnary.org/text o_soul_are_you_weary_and_troubled.

CHAPTER 4: JESUS, THE LIVING WATER

1. Aron Ralston, "Trapped," Outside, September 1, 2004, https://www.outsideonline.com/outdoor-adventure/exploration-survival/trapped/.

2. *Encyclopedia Britannica*, s.v. "Siege of Jerusalem," https://www.britannica.com/event/Siege-of-Jerusalem-70.

3. Marc Chalufour, "What's behind Boom of Christianity in China?" The Brink, February 2, 2023, https://www.bu.edu/articles/2023/why-is-christianity-growing-in-china/.

4. See, for example, Mark Bradley, *Too Many to Jail: The Story of Iran's New Christians* (Oxford: Monarch Books, 2014), 36; and Stoyan Zaimov, "Iran Is Witnessing 'One of Fastest Growing Church

Movements,' but Christians Face Intense Persecution," *Christian Post* October 16, 2018, http://www.christianpost.com/news/iran-is -witnessing-one-of-fastest-growing-church-movements-but-christians -face-intense-persecution.html.

CHAPTER 6: JESUS, THE SERVANT

1. Isabelle Casey, "King Charles Makes Incredibly Generous Promise to Staff During Cost of Living Crisis," *Hello*, November 12, 2022, https:// www.hellomagazine.com/royalty/20221112156856/king-charles -generous-gesture-staff/.

CHAPTER 7: JESUS, THE LIGHT IN THE DARKNESS

1. Mike Valerio, "Trapped in the Darkness: First-Hand Look at Underground Cave Conditions," July 8, 2018, WUSA 9, https://www .wusa9.com/article/news/local/virginia/trapped-in-the-darkness-first -hand-look-at-underground-cave-conditions/65–571484901.
2. Josh Huynh, "Bob Newhart—Stop It," YouTube, September 2, 2010, https://www.youtube.com/watch?v=Ow0lr63y4Mw.

CONCLUSION

1. "Worship." *Merriam-Webster.com Dictionary*, Merriam-Webster, accessed November 3, 2023, https://www.merriam-webster.com /dictionary/worship.

ABOUT THE AUTHOR

P hil Robertson is a professional hunter who invented his own duck call and founded the successful Duck Commander company. He also starred in the popular television series on A&E, *Duck Dynasty*, and is now the cohost of the hugely popular podcast *Unashamed with Phil & Jase Robertson*. He is a *New York Times* bestselling author of *Uncanceled*; *Jesus Politics*; *The Theft of America's Soul*; *Happy, Happy, Happy*; and *UnPHILtered*. He and his wife, Kay, live in West Monroe, Louisiana. He has five children, nineteen grandchildren, and thirteen great-grandchildren.

BASED ON THE INSPIRING TRUE STORY THAT STARTED A DYNASTY

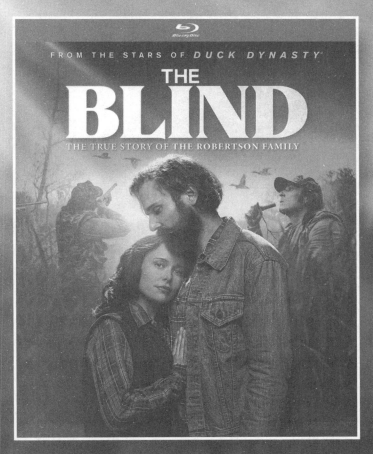

Long before Phil Robertson (*Duck Dynasty*) became a reality TV star, he fell in love with Miss Kay and started a family, but his demons threatened to tear their lives apart. Set in the backwoods swamps of 1960s Louisiana, *The Blind* shares never-before-revealed moments in Phil's life as he seeks to conquer the shame of his past, ultimately finding redemption in an unlikely place.

PG-13 — PARENTS STRONGLY CAUTIONED — THEMATIC CONTENT AND SMOKING

AVAILABLE NOW ON BLU-RAY, DVD, AND DIGITAL